:30 MINUTE BRACELETS

:30 MINUTE BRACELETS

▶ 60 Quick & Creative Projects for Jewelers

Marthe Le Van

LARK CRAFTS
Asheville

Art Director
Kathleen Holmes

Art Production
Kay Holmes Stafford

Junior Designer
Carol Barnao

Editorial Assistants
Abby Haffelt
Hannah Doyle

Illustrator
Orrin Lundgren

Photographer
Stewart O'Shields

Cover Designer
Kay Holmes Stafford

An Imprint of Sterling Publishing
387 Park Avenue South
New York, NY 10016

If you have questions or comments about
this book, please visit: larkcrafts.com

Le Van, Marthe.
  30-minute bracelets : 60 quick & creative projects for jewelers / Marthe Le Van. -- 1st ed.
      p. cm. -- (30-minute series)
  ISBN 978-1-60059-488-5 (pbk.)
  1. Bracelets. 2. Jewelry making. I. Title. II. Title: Thirty-minute bracelets.
  TT212.L414 2012
  739.27--dc23
                              2011037359

10 9 8 7 6 5 4 3 2 1

First Edition

Published by Lark Crafts
An Imprint of Sterling Publishing Co., Inc.
387 Park Avenue South, New York, NY 10016

© 2012, Lark Crafts, an Imprint of Sterling Publishing Co., Inc

Distributed in Canada by Sterling Publishing,
c/o Canadian Manda Group, 165 Dufferin Street
Toronto, Ontario, Canada M6K 3H6

Distributed in the United Kingdom by GMC Distribution Services,
Castle Place, 166 High Street, Lewes, East Sussex, England BN7 1XU

Distributed in Australia by Capricorn Link (Australia) Pty Ltd.,
P.O. Box 704, Windsor, NSW 2756 Australia

Manufactured in China

ISBN 13: 978-1-60059-488-5

For information about custom editions, special sales, and premium and corporate purchases, please
contact Sterling Special Sales Department at 800-805-5489 or specialsales@sterlingpub.com.

Requests for information about desk and examination copies available to college and university professors
must be submitted to academic@larkbooks.com. Our complete policy can be found at www.larkcrafts.com.

CONTENTS

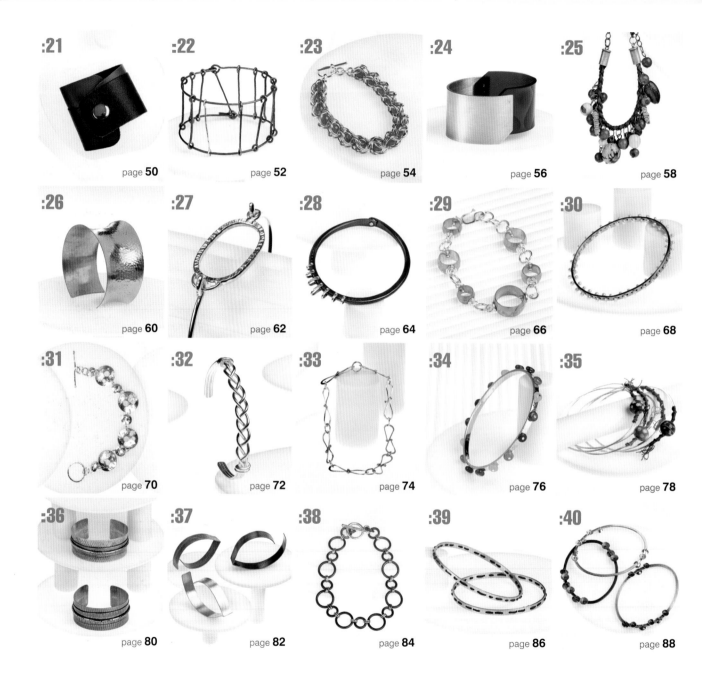

Introduction

You use your wrists all day. Why not take 30 minutes to craft a bracelet to adorn them? Let those wrists rest from the monotony of everyday chores, and treat them to a creative task—and a jewelry accessory! Whether they'll jangle, clink, sparkle, or shine, your hand-crafted bracelets will accent this already expressive body part.

So take just 30 minutes—every day, once a week, once a month, or whenever the urge hits you—and dedicate them to crafting your new favorite bracelet. The variety of materials and styles in *30-Minute Bracelets* ensures you'll have a heap of fun projects to choose from. You'll also have many chances to test and improve skills, such as hammering, drilling, soldering, and adding patinas. From Nancy Lee's copper sheet metal cuff (page 34) to Ann Lumsden's jade-studded silver bangle (page 77), *30-Minute Bracelets* offers a wide range of wearable projects—some elegant or playful, others eccentric or stylish—a bracelet for every side of you.

30-Minute Bracelets offers designs for all skill levels. Tap into your wild side with Victoria Takahashi's drilled antler and black diamond chain bracelet (page 40). In this project you'll practice drilling, forging, tube riveting, and wirework, resulting in an edgy bracelet with naturally shed antler tip as its centerpiece. Let your avant-garde and classic sensibilities mingle: with Isabella Lamontagne's rod-punctuated silver cuff (page 121), there's no need to sacrifice eccentricity for elegance. In this project you'll practice sawing, drilling, riveting, forming, solder-ing, and finishing, creating sloping rows of rods for a novel, kinetic twist on an otherwise timeless cuff. Or channel your inner child with Amy Tavern's colorful yarn-wrapped bangles (page 110). In this project you'll practice soldering, forming wire, and textile wrapping, and you'll end up with a set of bright, fresh bangles perfect for any occasion. With *30-Minute Bracelets'* wide array of projects, you can find a look for any season, event, setting, or mood.

As you thumb through the book, you'll notice its time-driven organiza-tion: under **Get Ready**, you'll find a short list of skills needed for the project (like wirework, soldering, or forging); under **Get Set**, you'll find the tools and materials needed to make it (like liver of sulfur, rivet wire, or waxed thread); and under **Go**, you'll find simple, thorough instruc-tions that guide you every step of the way.

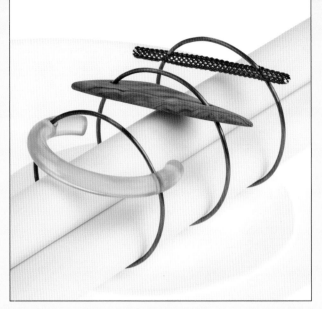

So don't waste another minute—take 30, set your clock, and **Get Ready, Get Set, Go!**

Bench Tool Kit

Bench pin

Steel bench block

Jeweler's saw frame

Saw blades

Beeswax

Needle files

Bastard file

Sandpaper, 200 and 400 grit

Emery paper

Chasing hammer

Rawhide or wooden mallet

Forging hammer

Mandrels

Dapping block and punches

Flexible shaft

Wood block

Drill bits

Burrs

Separating disc

Scribe

Stainless steel ruler

Dividers

Calipers

Pliers

Wire cutters

Center punch

Burnisher

Safety glasses

Safety gloves

Hearing protection

Dust mask

Soldering Kit

Soldering torch

Striker

Heat resistant soldering surfaces (charcoal blocks, firebricks, or ceramic plates)

Flux

Flux brush or other applicator

Solder (hard, medium, and easy)

Snips

Small embroidery scissors

Solder pick

Tweezers

Cross-locking tweezers with wooden handle

Third hand

Copper tongs

Water for quenching

Pickle

Pickle warming pot

Safety glasses

Fire extinguisher

:01 → Get Ready

SAWING • FILING • HAMMERING • BENDING

▶▶ ▶ Get Set

Brass sheet, 20 gauge,
10½ x ¾ inch
(26.7 x 1.9 cm)

Bench tool kit, page 9

Photocopied design
template ❶
enlarge 200%

FINISHED SIZE
6.5 x 6 x 2 cm

▶ ▶ ▶ Go

1. Saw a 10½ x ¾-inch (26.7 x 1.9 cm) band from the brass sheet. Mark the middle of the band, and saw out the shape following the photocopied design template. File the metal edges smooth.

2. Add texture and shape to the band by hammering it with the ball side of a chasing hammer on top of a steel block. Do not hammer the last 1½ inches (3.8 cm) on each end of the band.

3. Place the band on a bracelet mandrel, and hammer it with a rawhide hammer to form the cuff shape.

4. Curl each end of the cuff inward with round-nose pliers to form an attractive curve.

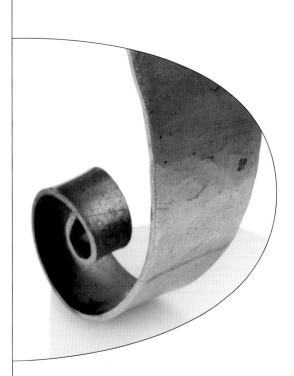

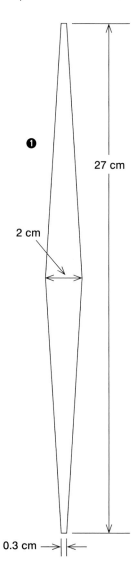

❶

27 cm

2 cm

0.3 cm

WITHDRAWN

:02

▶ Get Set

Leather, medium weight,
2 x 6½ inches
(5.1 x 16.5 cm)

Heavyweight thread
for leather

Sewing needle

Leather glue

3 sterling silver strips,
1 x 4 mm, each 6 inches
(15.2 cm)

Scribe

Toothpick

Plastic mallet

FINISHED SIZE
5.1 x 16.5 cm

▶ ▶ ▶ Go

1. Cut two leather rectangles using a sharp craft knife, each 2 x 6½ inches (5.1 x 16.5 cm).

2. Mark locations to be pierced on one leather rectangle. Cut each mark with a craft knife.

3. Spread a thin layer of glue on the back of both leather rectangles, avoiding the areas where the metal will be woven. Put the two glued sides together, and let dry.

4. Use a needle and thread or a sewing machine to stitch the pieces together, 5 mm from the edge.

5. Horizontally thread each sterling silver strip through the cuts in the leather. Make sure to alternate the pattern, creating a checkerboard effect.

6. Form the shape of the cuff by hand. Hammer with a mallet on an oval bracelet mandrel to harden the silver strips.

Want to make another bracelet?

The yellow cuff is a slight variation on these instructions, using decorative brads. Make holes in the leather, insert a mini brad through each, and flare the ends on the reverse side. Spread glue on one side of a second leather rectangle and on the back of the leather with the brads. Adhere the glued sides together, and let dry. Stitch around the cuff and add a snap to finish.

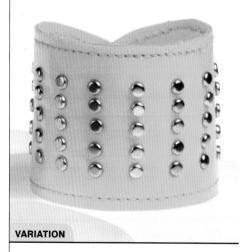

VARIATION

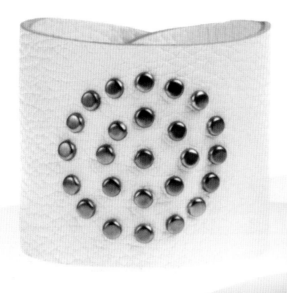

:03

Get Ready

ROLLER PRINTING • **SAWING** • **FILING** • **POLISHING** • **GLUING**

▶ ▶ Get Set

Sterling silver sheet,
    18 gauge,
    ¾ x 2¼ inches
    (1.9 x 5.7 cm)

Patterned ribbon,
    10 mm wide, 5 inches
    (12.7 cm) long

Sterling silver chain ends,
    10 mm

Sterling silver lobster clasp

Iron-on fabric adhesive

Bench tool kit, page 9

Clothing iron

Epoxy

FINISHED SIZE
19.5 x 1 x 1.5 cm

▶ ▶ ▶ Go

1. Transfer an enlarged version of the ribbon pattern onto heavyweight paper. This can be done freehand or you can scan and enlarge an image of the ribbon and print it directly on the paper.

2. Cut out the areas of the ribbon pattern that will be raised on the embossed metal.

3. Center the paper cut-out on the polished silver surface. Place a plain piece of the same paper on the back surface, sandwiching the silver between the two pieces of paper. Roller print the silver. Once the silver has been embossed, protect its front surface with clear tape.

4. Mark and cut a rectangle from the silver sheet that is approximately 1.5 x 5.5 cm. File and sand the edges.

5. Mark and cut a narrow slot at each end of the rectangle, just large enough for the ribbon to pass through. Use needle files to smooth the metal edges.

6. Polish the edges of the silver piece, taking care not to polish the front surface. Rub the front surface face down on a polishing cloth to shine the raised surfaces, while leaving the recessed areas matte.

7. Cut two pieces of ribbon, each approximately 5 inches (12.7 cm) long. Thread one ribbon through each slot in the silver and fold it in half.

8. Cut two strips of iron-on fabric adhesive that are slightly narrower than the ribbon. Follow the manufacturer's directions to adhere the folded ribbons together.

9. Cut the two ribbons to the desired length. Use epoxy to adhere the silver end tabs to the ribbons. Attach the lobster clasp to complete the bracelet.

→▶ **Get Set**

54 turquoise gemstone chips, 5 to 8 mm

60 gold seed beads, size 11

Gold-colored toggle clasp, 10 mm

2 thread protectors, gold tone

Fine beading thread, one spool

Beading needle

Scissors

FINISHED SIZE
1.3 x 19 cm

▶▶▶ **Go**

1. Thread a beading needle with approximately 4¼ feet (1.25 m) of beading thread.

2. Pass a thread protector through the ring on one end of the toggle clasp. Leaving about 6 inches (15.2 cm) as a tail, thread through one seed bead, through the protector, and back through the seed bead. Repeat this process once, and then thread five seed beads, pull the thread up, and add three turquoise chips. Start the sequence: string six seed beads, and then three turquoise chips. Repeat this sequence eight times, making nine repeats.

3. String six seed beads. Pass a thread protector through the ring on the other part of the toggle clasp. Pass the thread through the protector and the last seed bead strung. Pass through the protector and the last bead again.

4. Pass the thread back through the next five seed beads. Pull up the thread and add three turquoise chips next to the previous three chips. Circle the thread through all six chips, and pull tight so the chips sit close together. Pass through the next six seed beads. Repeat this sequence eight times.

5. At last seed bead, pass through the thread protector and pass both ends of the thread back to the middle of the first set of chips. Pull the thread tight, knot, and trim the ends.

▶▶ ▶ Get Set

Silver-plated pewter toggle,
   1½ inches (3.8 cm)
   in diameter

6 aluminum jump rings,
   18 gauge, ⅛-inch
   (3 mm) ID (interior
   diameter)

4 aluminum jump rings,
   18 gauge, ⁵⁄₃₂-inch
   (4 mm) ID (interior
   diameter)

39 black anodized
   aluminum jump rings,
   16 gauge, ⁵⁄₁₆-inch
   (8 mm) ID (interior
   diameter)

78 black/gunmetal
   anodized aluminum
   leaf-shaped
   components

2 pairs of flat-nose pliers

FINISHED SIZE
24.1 x 3.8 x 1.3 cm

▶▶ ▶ Go

1. Use both pairs of pliers to twist open all of the jump rings. Weave a 18-gauge, ⅛-inch (3 mm) ID jump ring through each of the loops at the end of the ring part of the toggle clasp. Close both rings.

2. Use a 16-gauge, ⁵⁄₁₆-inch (8 mm) ID black jump ring to pick up two of the leaf-shaped components so that the concave sides face each other. Weave this ring through one of the 18-gauge, ⅛-inch (3 mm) ID jump rings attached to the clasp. Twist the 16-gauge ring closed.

3. With a new 16-gauge ring, pick up two more leaves with the concave sides facing each other. Separate the two leaves on the 16-gauge ring you added on the last step. Weave the open ring through the 16-gauge ring added on the last step—making sure to weave between the leaves—and close. Repeat this step once more.

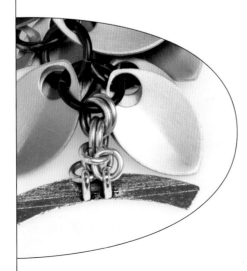

4. Repeat steps 2 and 3 on the other 18-gauge, ⅛-inch (3 mm) ID ring attached to the clasp so you have a chain of three rings with leaves hanging from each small ring on the clasp.

5. Pick up two more leaves with an open 16-gauge ring. Weave the open ring through the last ring on each of the three-link chains you created in steps 2 through 4, making sure to separate the two leaves on each ring and weave between them. Twist closed the new ring.

6. Repeat steps 2 through 5 on the single ring connecting the two chains of three rings. This time, however, make sure to create two chains that are four rings long instead of three.

7. Repeat steps 2 through 6 so that you have two alternating sets of three-link chains and four-link chains, each link with two dangling leaves on it. Add another set of two three-link chains to the last single ring, and then connect these with a single 16-gauge ring with two leaves.

8. Connect two 18-gauge, ³⁄₁₆-inch (5 mm) ID rings to the 16-gauge ring at the end of the bracelet, making sure to weave on the rings in between the two leaves. Connect another two 18-gauge, ³⁄₁₆-inch (5 mm) ID rings to the 18-gauge rings you just added. To these rings, connect two 18-gauge, ⅛-inch (3 mm) rings. Use another open 18-gauge, ⅛-inch (3 mm) ID ring to connect each of these 18-gauge, ⅛-inch (3 mm) ID rings to each loop of the bar part of the clasp.

:06 ▶ Get Ready

**PIERCING AND SAWING • FILING • SANDING • DRILLING
USING LIVER OF SULFUR • RIVETING WITH SPACERS**

▶▶ Get Set

Copper sheet, 20 gauge,
 4¾ x 4¾ inches
 (12 x 12 cm)

Aluminum sheet, 20 gauge,
 4¾ x 4¾ inches
 (12 x 12 cm)

Copper tubing, 3 mm OD
 (outside diameter),
 2 inches (5.1 cm)

Aluminum tubing, 2.3 mm
 OD (outside diameter),
 3½ inches (8.9 cm)

Bench tool kit, page 9

Tubing cutter

Sealing wax

Photocopied design
 template ❶
 enlarge 200%

FINISHED SIZE
10.5 x 10.5 x 0.6 cm

▶▶▶ Go

1. Using photocopied template 1, cut out the shape from the copper sheet. Pierce and saw out the interior circle. File and sand the exterior and interior edges.

2. Repeat step 1 to cut out and finish the aluminum shape.

3. Use a tube cutter or a jeweler's saw to cut the copper tubing into 12 pieces, each 4 mm long. Cut the aluminum tubing into 12 pieces, each 7 mm long.

4. Tape the two metal triangles together, making sure the circles in the center are perfectly aligned. Using photocopied template 1 as a guide, center punch 12 locations for riveting the aluminum sheet. Using a 2.3-mm bit, drill a hole at each dimple. Remove the tape and remove any burrs with 400-grit sandpaper.

5. Patina the copper triangle and tubing with liver of sulfur. Seal the surface with paste wax.

6. Feed each aluminum tube into a copper tube.

7. Place the copper triangle on an anvil and insert one pair of tubes into corresponding holes in the copper and aluminum. Rivet. Insert another pair of tubes into the holes opposite the first rivet, and rivet. Continue riveting in this manner until each rivet is secure, and the two metal sheets are firmly joined.

❶

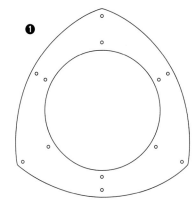

07

► Get Ready

BEADWEAVING THREE-BEAD NDEBELE/HERRINGBONE STITCH
BEADWEAVING LADDER STITCH • USING A TOGGLE LOOP

► ► Get Set

111 round beads,
  size 8/0, steel gray

116 cylinder beads,
  size 8/0, steel gray

14 round beads,
  size 15/0, steel gray

Magnetic ball clasp

Black beading thread,
  1 spool

Beading needle

Wax

FINISHED SIZE
20.3 cm long

DESIGNER'S NOTE

To create a more linear alignment of beads, securely add an additional thread that travels endlessly through the three stacks without transitions. This is best done prior to adding the clasp.

► ► ► Go

1. On a comfortable length of conditioned thread, form a ladder of three size 8/0 cylinder beads. Fold the beads over to join the open ends into the base row by passing through the first bead to the last bead of the ladder. Reweave leaving an 18-inch (45.7 cm) tail on the opposite side of the direction you are working. Note: Cylinders will be more stable as a base than round beads.

2. Pick up two size 8/0 round beads and needle down through the next adjacent bead. Work in one direction—either clockwise or counterclockwise.

3. Needle up through the next adjacent size 8/0 cylinder bead. Pick up one size 8/0 round bead and needle down through the next adjacent round bead of this row and down to the cylinder bead of the previous row.

4. Needle up through the next adjacent cylinder bead and through the round bead of the previous row. Pick up two cylinder beads and needle down through the next adjacent round bead and through to the cylinder bead below.

5. Needle up through the next adjacent cylinder bead and through the round bead of the previous row. Pick up one cylinder bead, and needle down through the next adjacent cylinder bead and through to the round bead below.

6. Needle up through the next adjacent round bead and through the cylinder bead of the previous row. Pick up two round beads, and needle down through the next adjacent cylinder bead and through to the round bead below.

7. Needle up through the next adjacent round bead and through the cylinder bead of the previous row. Pick up one round bead and needle down through the next adjacent round bead and through to the cylinder bead below.

8. Repeat steps 4 through 7 until you reach the desired length. End the work with a row of size 8/0 round beads.

9. With the needle coming up from the stack, needle down into the next adjacent bead, and travel down the stack 10 beads. Exit a bead, and travel back up in the center core of the three-bead stacks.

10. Exiting the center of the three-bead core, needle over, and then go under each thread bridge between the size 8/0 round beads. This will cinch the thread bridges and center the thread.

11. Pick up one size 8/0 round bead, four size 15/0 round beads, one side of the magnetic clasp, and three size 15/0 round beads. Pass back down through the first size 15/0 round bead and through the size 8/0 round bead, forming a loop.

12. Traveling out of the loop, repeat step 10 and travel through the loop to reinforce. Travel down a stack of beads, reweaving the end of the thread to secure it by passing between stacks as you travel. Trim the end when you are finished.

13. Create a loop at the opposite end of the work by repeating steps 2 and 3 at the base row using the tail. Repeat steps 9 through 13 to finish.

08

► Get Ready

►► Get Set

Lumber toggle
  and lumber links

2 brass jump rings,
  16 gauge, each 12 mm

Brass jump ring,
  16 gauge, 15 mm

4 brass jump rings,
  16 gauge, each 9 mm

8 etched brass jump rings,
  16 gauge, each 9 mm

Brass jump ring,
  16 gauge, 6 mm

6 red jasper rectangular
  brick beads,
  each 12 mm

6 bronze round wires,
  20 gauge,
  each 2 inches
  (5.1 cm)

Cotton, hemp, or waxed
  linen cord, 36 inches
  (91.5 cm)

3 brass eye pins,
  22 gauge,
  each 1½ inches
  (3.8 cm)

3 glass flower beads,
  each 5 mm

Round-nose pliers

FINISHED SIZE
1.3 x 20.3 cm

►►► Go

1. Cut a length of cotton hemp cord or natural colored string 10 to 12 inches (25.4 to 30.5 cm) long. Hold one end against a 15-mm plain brass jump ring, and start wrapping the cord tightly around the ring. When you have wrapped the cord completely around the ring with no gaps, securely tie the cord in an overhand knot. Trim the ends, leaving tails of about ½ inch (1.3 cm). Repeat this step for the two remaining 12-mm plain brass jump rings.

2. Using round-nose pliers, make a wrapped loop on one end of a 2-inch (5.1 cm) length of bronze wire. Thread a jasper rectangular bead onto the wire, and make a wrapped loop on the other end. Repeat this step for the remaining five rectangular brick beads.

3. Open all remaining jump rings.

4. Connect the bracelet in the following order, closing the jump rings as you go:

Lumber toggle
9-mm etched jump ring
Cord-wrapped jump ring
9-mm etched jump ring
9-mm plain jump ring
3 beaded links
9-mm plain jump ring
9-mm etched jump ring
Lumber link
9-mm etched jump ring
Cord-wrapped jump ring
9-mm etched jump ring
9-mm plain jump ring
3 beaded links
9-mm plain jump ring
9-mm etched jump ring
Lumber link
9-mm etched jump ring
Cord-wrapped jump ring
9-mm etched jump ring
6-mm plain jump ring
Toggle bar closure

5. Using brass eye pins, make a wrapped-loop dangle for each glass flower bead. Connect two flower beads to one 9-mm plain jump ring in the center of the bracelet. Add one flower bead to another 9-mm plain jump ring.

:09

▶▶ Get Set

2 sterling silver sheets,
   22 gauge,
   each 1½ x ⁵⁄₁₆ inch
   (3.8 x 0.8 cm)

Copper sheet, 20 gauge,
   1½ x ⁵⁄₁₆ inch
   (3.8 x 0.8 cm)

Copper tubing, 3.2 mm

Sterling silver rollo chain,
   5 mm, 6 inches
   (15.2 cm)

3 sterling silver jump rings,
   18 gauge, each 3.5 mm

Sterling silver lobster clasp,
   10 x 6 mm

Bench tool kit, page 9

Photocopied design
   template ❶

FINISHED SIZE
20.3 x .6 cm

▶▶▶ Go

1. Apply a rough sanded finish to one side of each silver sheet. Apply a file finish to both sides of the copper sheet.

2. Use the photocopied design templates to pierce and saw the designs from the silver and copper sheets. File and sand each metal piece.

3. Drill a 3-mm hole in the center of one silver piece, 3 mm from the end.

4. Using the drilled silver piece from step 3 as a template, drill a 3-mm hole on the remaining sheet metal pieces. De-burr the holes.

5. Cut two 4-mm pieces of ⅛-inch (3 mm) copper tubing.

6. Stack the metal sheets with the copper in the middle and the rough-sanded sides of the silver facing out. Tube rivet the metal through the drilled holes.

7. Drill a matching hole on the opposite end of the metal through all three layers. Tube rivet this side of the stack. To finish the tube rivets, gently hammer them with the round face of a chasing hammer.

8. File all sides of the metal flush. Slightly round the corners of the piece and bevel the edges.

9. Cut two 3-inch (7.6 cm) lengths of the rollo chain. Use jump rings to attach the chain to the sheet metal through the tube rivets. Use the remaining silver jump ring to attach the lobster clasp.

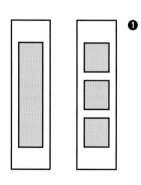

❶

:10

►► ► Get Set

14 carbon steel internal retaining rings with black phosphate coating, each ½ inch (1.3 cm) bore diameter

15 bronze jump rings, each 5 mm

Small copper toggle clasp

2 pairs of chain-nose pliers

FINISHED SIZE
2.5 x 17.8 cm

►► ► Go

1. Arrange a retaining ring on your work surface so that it resembles a backwards C. Arrange a second retaining ring above the first but facing the opposite direction. The two retaining rings form an S, and the same side is facing up. (One side of the retaining ring will be flat and the other will have a slight curve on the surface. This may be easier to feel than to see.)

2. Using both pairs of needle-nose pliers, one in each hand, open a jump ring. Thread the jump ring through the top hole of the bottom retaining ring, front to back. Thread the same jump ring through the bottom hole of the top retaining ring, back to front. Using both pairs of pliers, close the jump ring so the two ends of the jump ring are flush and the two retaining rings are connected in the middle of the S.

3. Arrange the next retaining ring so that it faces the same direction as the first retaining ring. Open a second jump ring and thread it through the second hole of the second retaining ring and the first hole of the third retaining ring. Close the jump ring.

4. Repeat this process until all retaining rings are connected in an undulating line with jump rings.

5. Use a jump ring to connect the toggle ring to the first retaining ring. Use a jump ring to connect the toggle bar to the last retaining ring.

Want to make another bracelet?

As shown in the variations photo, alter the pattern by linking the retaining rings in the same direction.

The retaining rings come in a several colors. Alternate these colors or the color wire of your jump rings for a different look.

VARIATIONS

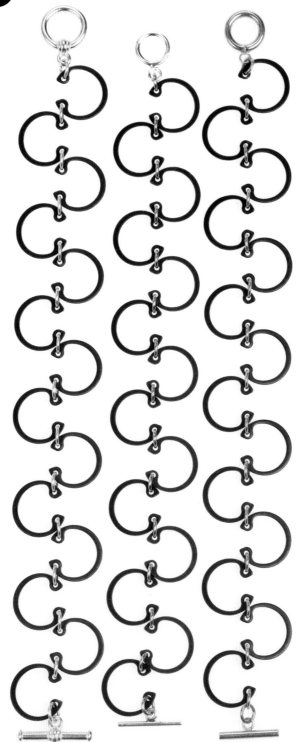

:11

▶ ▶ Get Set

Plastic folder, any color

Sterling silver round wire, 18 gauge, 1 inch (2.5 cm)

Sterling silver disk, 22 gauge, ¼ inch (6 mm)

Sterling silver tube, 1 mm ID (interior diameter), 2.05 mm OD (outside diameter), 7.12 mm long

Solvent inkpad

Rubber stamp

Bench tool kit, page 9

Soldering kit, page 9

FINISHED SIZE
7 x 7 x 3.8 cm

▶ ▶ ▶ Go

1. Use scissors to cut the folder into six plastic strips, each ½ x 8¼ inches (1.3 x 21 cm) long.

2. Line up the strips on a flat surface in parallel rows, and tape them down. Using the inkpad and a rubber stamp, create a pattern on the strips. Once the ink dries, seal it with matte spray fixative.

3. Use a permanent marker to mark the center of one end of each strip, 5 mm from the edge. Mark a spot on the opposite end of each strip that is slightly off center, 5 mm from the edge. Round the ends with scissors, or snip each corner at an angle.

4. Use a torch to ball one end of the 1-inch (2.5 cm) 18-gauge wire.

5. Thread the wire through a corresponding hole in a drawplate. Use a chasing hammer to flatten the ball, making a headpin.

6. Drill a 1-mm hole in the ¼-inch (6 mm) silver disk. Drill a 1-mm hole at each marked spot on the strips.

7. Gather the strips together. Thread the headpin through one hole at a time, making sure to overlap the strips in a pleasing manner and to secure each strip in a complete circle. Thread the drilled ¼-inch (6 mm) disk onto the headpin, and trim the remaining wire to a good length for riveting. Rivet the wire.

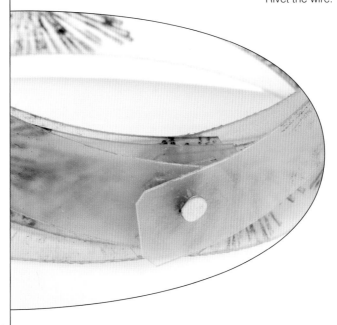

DESIGNER: **JUNGWHA KIM**

→ Get Ready

**PIERCING AND SAWING • DRILLING • USING LIVER OF SULFUR
RIVETING • FORMING**

→► Get Set

Copper sheet, 20 gauge,
6 x 2 inches
(15.2 x 5.1 cm)

Sterling silver sheet,
24 gauge, 6 x 2 inches
(15.2 x 5.1 cm)

Sterling silver wire,
18 gauge, 1 inch
(2.5 cm)

Bench tool kit, page 9

Microcrystalline
sealing wax

Photocopied design
template ❶

FINISHED SIZE
6 x 4 x 4 cm

→►► Go

1. Use photocopied template 1 to saw out the shape from the copper sheet. Use the same template to saw out the pierced shape from the silver sheet. File and sand each edge.

2. Place the sterling oval on top of the copper one. Tape them together. Following design template 1, center punch the 10 locations for the rivet holes. Drill the four center holes with a 1-mm bit. Remove any burrs using 400-grit sandpaper.

3. Cut a 3-mm piece of 18-gauge silver wire for each rivet. File both ends of the rivet wires.

4. Patina the copper oval using liver of sulfur, and seal the surface with paste wax.

5. Place the copper and sterling silver ovals together and rivet the four center rivets.

6. Using a rawhide mallet, bend the ovals into a bracelet form around a bracelet mandrel.

7. Drill the remaining holes through the metal and finish riveting on the bracelet mandrel.

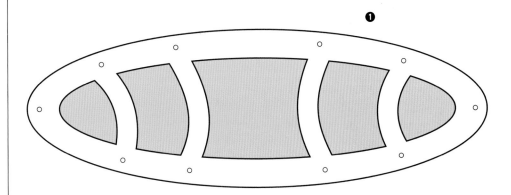

❶

:13

▶▶ ▶ Get Set

Copper sheet, 22 gauge,
   3 x 9 inches
   (7.6 x 22.9 cm)

Brown paper towel

Manila file folder

Bench tool kit, page 9

Soldering kit, page 9

Microcrystalline
   sealing wax

Photocopied design
   template ❶
   enlarge 200%

FINISHED SIZE
6.5 x 17.1 cm

DESIGNER'S NOTE
If a rolling mill is not
available, use a texturing
hammer to texture the metal
after it has been annealed.

▶▶ ▶ Go

1. Using a scribe, transfer the photocopied design template onto the copper sheet. Cut out the design using metal shears or a saw. File and sand the copper strip to a 400-grit finish.

2. Anneal the metal, allowing the torch flame to turn the copper bright orange-red in places, and then quench immediately in cold water. (This is your patina, so be sure you are happy with it before you continue.) Do not pickle. Dry the piece well.

3. Select a brown paper towel to use as a texture for roller printing. Cut or tear the paper to fit over the copper.

4. Cut two pieces of manila file folder to fit over the copper. Make a rolling mill "sandwich" in this order: file folder, texture paper, copper, and file folder.

5. Place the sandwich in the rolling mill, short end first, and roll through. Turn the sandwich around and feed through again, keeping the same side on top each time.

6. To create the scroll, hold the copper strip with the patterned side toward you. Using round-nose pliers and your fingers, gently roll the wide inside edge of the bracelet toward the patterned side. Minimal use of pliers creates a smoother look. Using the same method, roll the narrow edge to a lesser degree.

7. Place the rolled copper strip on the bracelet mandrel, and hammer it with a rawhide mallet. Make adjustments to the scroll as desired.

8. Sand the high points of the metal with 400-grit sandpaper. Wash and then wax the bracelet. Buff it with a clean, soft cloth.

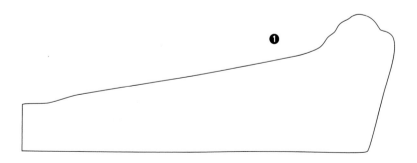

:14

▶▶ Get Set

Sterling silver flat wire,
  2 x 8 mm, 10 inches
  (25.4 cm)

Sterling silver round wire,
  14 gauge, 2 inches
  (5.1 cm)

Bench tool kit, page 9

Torch

FINISHED SIZE
7.8 cm in diameter

▶▶▶ Go

1. Cut the flat silver wire into four 2½-inch (6.4 cm) sections. File the wire ends flat and round the corners.

2. Mark and dimple a center point on each wire end, 3 mm from the edge. Drill each location with a 1.95-mm bit. Use a round ball burr to countersink each drilled hole.

3. Snip the 14-gauge round wire into four pieces. Ball one end of each piece of wire.

4. Attach two sections of flat wire with a balled round wire. Ball the other end of the wire, making sure the ball firmly holds the flat wires together.

5. Attach the remaining flat wires in the same manner described in step 4, making sure one end of each wire is under the previous wire, and one end is on top of the next one. Making these connections will give the bangle its shape.

6. Hammer each ball on the inside of the bangle flat with the round face of a ball peen hammer. This action should also flatten the ball on the outside of the bangle.

7. Use a heatless grinding wheel to remove the flattened wire balls, and sand the areas until smooth.

8. Finish the bangle by brushing it with a steel brush.

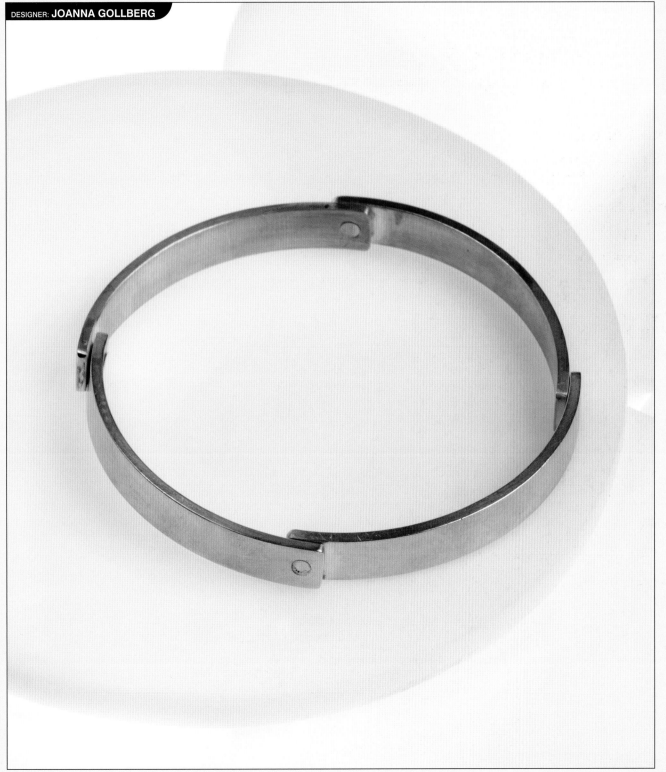

⇢ ▶ **Get Set**

7 sterling silver jump rings, 18 gauge, between 10 and 15 mm, hammered flat

Sterling silver disk, 20 gauge, 8 mm

Super-fine copper thread, 1 cone

Sterling silver crimp bead, 2 mm

Bench tool kit, page 9

Soldering kit, page 9

2 push pins

Stainless steel flexible magnetic needle

FINISHED SIZE
6½ inches (16.5 cm)

DESIGNER'S NOTE
The copper thread is extremely fine and can be difficult to handle. To make winding the thread around the pushpins easier, use two or three cones at the same time.

⇢ ▶ ▶ **Go**

1. Make a button by drilling a 1.6-mm hole in the center of the silver disk.

2. Solder each 18-gauge jump ring together. Hammer the silver flat with a flat-faced hammer on a steel block.

3. Press two pushpins into a wooden surface, 32 inches (82 cm) apart. Loop the copper thread around the pushpins 50 times. Gently remove the pins, cut both ends of the threads, and tie a slip knot at the 15-inch (38 cm) mark. Put a pushpin through the slip knot, and tighten it. Push the pin into the bench to secure the threads.

4. Make the loop for the clasp by dividing the threads into three equal amounts. Braid these strands together for 1¼ inches (3 cm). Remove the pin from the bench, and gently tug on the short end to release the knot.

Push the pin back into the bench, and loop the braided segment around it. Gather all the threads together, and divide into three equal strands.

5. Braid the copper threads for 1 inch (2.5 cm). Thread one jump ring through the rightmost strand section, and push it up against the braid. Continue braiding for a length equal to the diameter of the jump ring. Pass the rightmost strand back through the jump ring, and braid for another 5 mm. Pick up another jump ring, and continue working. Repeat this process until all seven jump rings are braided into the bracelet. Braid for an additional 1 inch (2.5 cm).

6. Gather all the copper strands together, and make an overhand knot against the end of the braid. Thread the strand through the large eye of the needle, and pass it through the buttonhole drilled in step 1. Make another overhand knot, and press it against the button to secure.

7. Thread the crimp bead, and push it against the knot. Crimp the bead, and trim the thread.

Want to make another bracelet?

Make a bracelet with a very thick braid.

Thread pearls or beads through one or more of the strands, and braid them into the bracelet.

Get Ready

DRILLING · SAWING · TUBE RIVETING · WIREWORK

▶ Get Set

Naturally shed antler tip,
3 inches (7.6 cm)

Sterling silver rollo chain,
5 mm, 5 to 6 inches
(12.7 to 15.2 cm)

Sterling silver rollo chain,
2 mm, 7 inches
(17.8 cm)

Sterling silver tubing,
4 mm OD (outside
diameter), 1½ inches
(3.8 cm)

Sterling silver lobster clasp
and ring

Sterling silver jump ring,
20 gauge, 3 mm

Sterling silver wire,
28 gauge, 3 inches
(7.6 cm)

5 rough black diamonds
or any beads,
each 2 to 3 mm

2 decorative top beads,
each 3 to 4 mm

2 sterling silver nail-head
headpins, 18 gauge

Bench tool kit, page 9

FINISHED SIZE
8 x 7 x 2 cm

▶ ▶ ▶ Go

1. Mark the antler tip where you will drill your two connecting holes. Drill 1.5-mm starter holes first, and then 4-mm holes.

2. Cut the 4-mm silver tubing to the appropriate length for making two tube rivets through the antler. Rivet each tube in place.

3. Slip a decorative top bead onto each headpin, thread one through each tube rivet, and make a loop on the end of each headpin with round-nose pliers. Attach 5½ inches (14 cm) of the 5-mm rollo chain to one loop, and add the clasp to the end of the chain.

4. Cut five different lengths of the 2-mm rollo chain. Add these to the clasp jump ring, and add the clasp jump ring to the remaining loop on the antler.

5. Cut five lengths of 28-gauge sterling silver wire, and ball one end of each. Thread a black diamond bead on each wire, make a loop with round-nose pliers, and then wrap the tail around the wire. Thread each of these onto the 3-mm silver jump ring, and add the jump ring to the same loop that holds the clasp ring.

6. Patina the bracelet, taking care to avoid touching the antler with any chemicals.

:17

▶ Get Ready

WIREWORK · BEADING · FORMING

▶ ▶ Get Set

Silver-plated copper
round wire, 14 gauge,
19 inches (48.3 cm)

4 two-holed sterling
silver spacers,
each 4 x 7 x 1 mm

4 sterling silver beads,
each 4 x 7 mm

2 sterling silver beads,
each 4 x 3 mm

66 square seed beads,
each 4 mm, two colors

1 faceted round bead,
7 mm

1 crystal bead, 5 mm

1 decorative sterling silver
bead, 2.5 x 5 mm

1 sterling silver headpin

Wire snips

Round-nose pliers

FINISHED SIZE
8 x 6.5 x 1.5 cm

▶ ▶ ▶ Go

1. Use snips to cut 7 inches (17.8 cm) of wire. Bend the wire in half using the largest curvature of the round-nose pliers. To create the catch, hold the wire ½ inch (1.3 cm) from the initial curve, and bend the wire at a 90-degree angle to the curve.

2. Thread a two-holed spacer bead onto the wire. Push the bead down the wire until it is ½ inch (1.3 cm) away from the point where the wire begins to curve.

3. Add seven square beads to each wire end, alternating colors to create a checkerboard pattern. Add one 4 x 7-mm bead to each wire and then a two-holed spacer bead. Use round-nose pliers to make a simple 5-mm loop in the end of each wire end. Position the loop at a 90-degree angle to the plane of the catch.

4. Bend the remaining 12-inch (30.5 cm) wire in half, using the largest curvature of the round-nose pliers. Use round-nose pliers and your fingers to make a large loop that measures ⅞ x ½ inch (2.2 x 1.3 cm).

5. Thread a two-holed spacer bead on the long wire ends. Push the bead up the wire until it rests next to the large loop created in step 4. Add beads to both ends of the wire form in the following order. (All square beads are strung in a checkerboard pattern.)

> 7 square beads
> 1 silver bead, 4 x 7 mm
> 1 two-holed spacer bead
>   (through both ends)
> 7 square beads
> 1 silver bead, 4 x 7 mm
> 7 square beads
> 1 silver bead, 4 x 7 mm
> 5 square beads
> 1 silver bead, 4 x 3 mm

6. Use round-nose pliers to make a 5-mm loop at the end of each wire and horizontal with the plane of the large loop. Use round-nose pliers to attach the two sets of loops at the end of the wires together.

7. Use the head pin to make a small dangle incorporating the 7-mm faceted round bead, the 2.5 x 5-mm sterling silver decorative bead, and the 5-mm crystal bead. Make a simple loop to attach the headpin to the large loop on the bracelet.

8. Hook the clasp together, and use your fingers to gently shape the bracelet into an oval.

DESIGNER: **KIMBERLY FISTLER**

DESIGNER: **KAREN J. LAUSENG**

:18

▶▶ ▶ **Get Set**

30–40 black sew-on snaps, size 1/0

100–120 sterling silver jump rings, 18 gauge, each 2.5 mm

Bench tool kit, page 9

FINISHED SIZE
6 x 4.7 x 0.7 cm

▶ ▶ ▶ **Go**

1. Unsnap three sew-on snaps. Using a jeweler's saw, cut a section of metal from one of the four narrow openings on the outer edge of the rim of the snap piece. Repeat this process with five snap pieces. File and sand the six cut sections, removing any sharp edges. Set aside.

2. Using two pairs of chain-nose pliers, open a jump ring, slide on one male and one female snap, and close the jump ring. Continue adding jump rings and snaps to create three chains of 20 snaps, alternating female and male snap sections. Make sure the snaps are all facing the same direction, with the recessed areas all on one side of the bracelet.

3. Connect the three chains of snaps with jump rings. Make sure the snaps are arranged so the male and female snaps create a checkerboard pattern. The finished bracelet will be three rows wide and 20 snaps long.

4. Use six jump rings to add the three cut snaps to each end of the bracelet. The cut areas should be at the very ends of the rows.

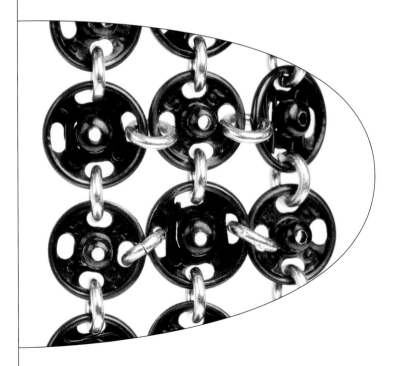

:19

Get Ready

**FINISHING • CUTTING • FILING • SANDING • FLARING
ANODIZING NIOBIUM (OPTIONAL) • STRINGING • SOLDERING**

Get Set

Niobium tubing, 3 mm,
5½ inches (14 cm)

34 large-hole sterling silver
beads, each 3 mm

Sterling silver curb chain,
1.2 mm, 7¼ inches
(18.4 cm)

2 sterling silver jump rings,
20 gauge, each 4 mm

Scrap wire, 28 to 30 gauge,
2 inches (5.1 cm)

Sterling silver lobster clasp,
6 mm

Bench tool kit, page 9

Soldering kit, page 9

Anodizing equipment
(optional)

FINISHED SIZE
16.5 cm

DESIGNER'S NOTE
You can buy pre-anodized
niobium tubing at jewelry
supply stores. You can
also make this bracelet
with sterling tubing and
different styles of beads
(see variation).

Go

1. Rub the niobium tubing with an abrasive pad to create an even, matte surface texture. The colors produced by the anodizing process appear best on this type of finish.

2. Cut the niobium tube into 16 pieces, each 8 mm in length. (A tube-cutting jig makes this easier, but if you don't have one, mark the length on the tube with dividers and saw through, making a straight cut.) File and sand the cut ends of the tubes.

3. Place the tubes on end on a steel block. Flare the ends of the tubes with a steel punch. Go slowly, flaring a bit at a time, and switching from end to end.

4. Clean the tubes in hot soapy water, rinse thoroughly, and don't touch them with your bare hands again before anodizing. High voltages are used in the anodizing process. Be sure to read and follow all the instructions and safety warnings that accompany your anodizing equipment. Anodize the flared tubes, experimenting with different voltages to achieve your desired colors.

5. Open the last link in the curb chain with the point of a scribe. Attach the lobster clasp to the end of the chain with a jump ring. Carefully solder the jump ring closed, and quickly quench in water to maintain the clasp's spring action. Clean and polish the jump ring and clasp.

6. Thread a very thin wire through the end link on the chain to help you string the sterling silver beads and niobium tubes. String on the beads and tubes, placing two beads at the ends of the bracelet and between each tube.

7. Thread another thin wire through the chain a few links past the final bead to hold everything in place, and cut off the excess chain. Note that when the chain is curved into a circle, the beads and tubes spread out, so make certain not to cut the chain too short.

8. Use the scribe to open the end chain link. Solder the second silver jump ring to the chain. Clean and polish the jump ring to complete the bracelet.

VARIATION

:20

⟶ Get Ready

SAWING • FILING • SANDING • DRILLING • SCORING AND BENDING
RIVETING • FORMING • USING NUTS AND BOLTS

⟶▶ Get Set

Nickel silver, 18 gauge,
9½ x 1 inch
(24.1 x 2.5 cm)

Vinyl record,
1¼ x 2¼ inches
(3.2 x 5.7 cm)

Miniature brass bolts
and nuts

Bench tool kit, page 9

Photocopied design
template ❶
enlarge 200%

FINISHED SIZE
6.4 x 7.6 x 6.4 cm

DESIGNER'S NOTE:
Use any item that can be
cold connected for the
decorative element.

▶▶▶ Go

1. Use photocopied template 1 to saw out the nickel silver shape. File, sand, and finish the edges, making sure to round the corners.

2. Sand the front and the back of the metal with 220-grit sandpaper.

3. Saw out the wedge of vinyl. Mark and drill the 1.18-mm holes in the vinyl element. File and sand the edges of the wedge.

4. Mark and drill corresponding 1.18-mm holes in the metal element.

5. Score a V groove in the metal along the dotted line on template 1 using the corner

of a triangular needle file and using a piece of scrap metal with a straight edge as a guide. Score one-half to two-thirds of the way through the metal. Finish filing with the corner of a square file to clean up and widen the groove.

6. Use your fingers to bend the long end of the metal into a slightly closed U shape. Form and refine the curve with a rawhide mallet and bracelet mandrel.

7. Bend the angle in the metal along the scored line. The metal should bend easily, resulting in a sharp bend.

8. Place the vinyl element on top of the metal, and assemble using the bolts and nuts.

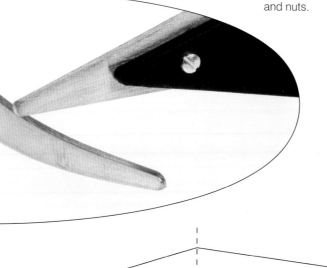

Approximately 3 inches (7.6 cm)
before rounding tip

Approximately 6½ inches (16.5 cm)
before rounding tip

❶

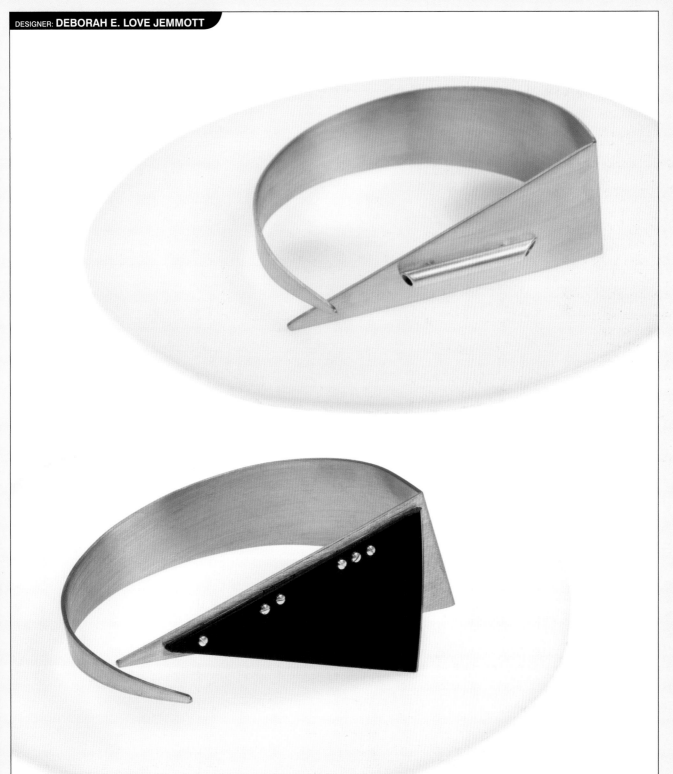

:21

▶ ▶ **Get Set**

2 pieces of stiff leather in contrasting colors

4-piece snap set

Awl

Craft knife

Punch, ⅛ inch (3 mm)

Rawhide mallet

Cutting mat

Snap setter and pedestal

Photocopied design template **❶** enlarge 200% on heavy stock paper

FINISHED SIZE
20.3 cm x 6.4 cm

DESIGNER'S NOTE
It's important that the leather isn't stretchy. Otherwise, the cuff will quickly lose its shape. Give your cuff extra stability by running a ¼-inch-wide (6 mm) piece of double-stick tape between the overlapping pieces of leather.

▶ ▶ ▶ **Go**

1. Use scissors to cut the photocopied templates from the heavy stock paper. Place the first piece of leather on the cutting board, good side up. Put the pattern on top, making sure the side labeled "Leather 1" is facing up. (Note: whichever leather you choose to be Leather 1 will be the predominant color shown on the finished cuff.)

2. Use a pencil to trace the pattern, and use an awl to poke a hole indicating the placement of snaps 1 and 2. Repeat this process with the second leather piece and the second design template, labeling this piece "Leather 2."

3. Cut out the leather, using a craft knife for the straight lines and scissors for the curves.

4. Use the punch and mallet to make the holes for the two snaps.

5. Lay the two pieces of leather on top of one another with the Snap 1 holes in alignment. Both pieces of leather should be facing right side up with Leather 1 on top. Insert the stud post into the hole and sandwich the bottom side with the stud. The stud should be flush on the leather with the post from the cap coming through it.

6. Turn the pieces over so everything is face down on your work surface, with the cap resting in the concave side of the setting pedestal. Place the end of the setter into the hole in the cap's post, and give one or two firm blows with the mallet.

7. Fan out the two leather pieces until the holes for Snap 2 line up. Sandwich the leather pieces between the remaining snap components. The post will be coming from the bottom side with the socket on top. These will be set on the flat side of the pedestal, with the cuff facing right side up. It will take several mallet blows to secure these pieces. Once the capped post is not jiggling around in the socket, the snap is properly set.

❶

⇢ ▶ **Get Set**

Steel wire, 16 gauge,
   49 inches (124.5 cm)

Brass wire, 16 gauge,
   2⅜ inches (6.1 cm)

Bench tool kit, page 9

Sealing wax

FINISHED SIZE
3.8 x 6.4 cm

DESIGNER'S NOTE
Measurements form a standard-size bangle. Adjust accordingly for smaller or larger sizes.

⇢ ▶ ▶ **Go**

1. Cut two 10-inch (25.4 cm) lengths of 16-gauge steel wire. At one end of each wire length, form a plain loop at the mid-point of the round-nose pliers. Planish the opposite wire end, and then hammer the full length of each wire.

2. Wrap each wire around the base of a bracelet mandrel so the hammered wire end overlaps the looped end by ¾ inch (1.9 cm). Mark the point of overlap with a white charcoal pencil, and bend a hook at this point on both bangles. The inner diameter of the bangles should be approximately 2½ inches (6.4 cm).

3. Fit the hook through the loop, and close the loop almost completely. Hammer the bangles flat, avoiding the hooks and loops.

4. Cut 11 lengths of steel wire and one length of brass wire, each 2⅜ inches (6.1 cm). Hammer each wire length.

5. Working near the tip of the round-nose pliers, form a plain loop at each end of all 2⅜-inch (6.1 cm) wire lengths. Make sure the loops lay flat.

6. Cut a 2⅛-inch (5.3 cm) length of steel wire. Form a plain loop at each end of this wire, using the very tip of the round-nose pliers. Make sure the loops lay flat. Connect these wire loops to the loops on the bangle, making sure the loop openings face inside the bangle.

7. Attach one loop of the remaining 11 wire components to each bangle. The components hold the bangles together, but all slide freely.

8. Clean the bracelet with steel wool, finish it with wax, and then buff.

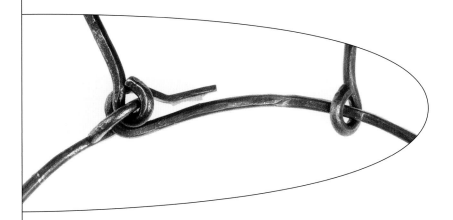

:23

→ **Get Ready**

CHAIN MAIL

▶▶▶ Get Set

64 aluminum jump rings,
18 gauge, ⁷⁄₁₆ inch
(1.1 cm)

6 aluminum jump rings,
18 gauge, ⅛ inch
(3 mm)

Silver toggle clasp, 8 mm

16 carnelian beads,
each 6 mm

Chain-nose or flat-nose
pliers, 2 pairs

FINISHED SIZE
20.3 x 0.6 x 0.6 cm

▶▶▶ Go

1. Open half of the large jump rings. Completely close the other half of the large jump rings.

2. Open five of the small jump rings. Completely close one of the small jump rings.

3. Place a small closed jump ring and the loop portion of the toggle clasp on a small open jump ring, and then close that jump ring.

4. Place two large closed jump rings on an open large jump ring. Weave the open jump ring through the small jump ring that is not attached to the toggle.

5. Double the single large open ring. That is, thread another open large jump ring through the two large closed rings and also through the small jump ring, and then close it. At this point, you should have the loop end of the toggle followed by two small jump rings followed by two doubled sets of large jump rings.

6. Hold the piece near the small jump rings so the small jump rings and the toggle are hanging at the bottom. Gently fold back the top large jump rings, and insert a bead between the two large jump rings at the bottom.

7. Bring the top-most large jump rings (bracketing the bead) back to meet at the center, and thread an open large jump ring through both of them. Note: Make sure that when you add a bead to each "cage" the jump rings do not get caught under the bead. They should bracket the bead on each side, hemming it in securely.

8. Add two closed jump rings to the open large jump ring, and then close the large jump ring. Double the open large jump ring through the two closed rings.

9. Repeat steps 6 through 8 until you've used all jump rings and beads or until the desired bracelet length is met.

10. To finish the bracelet, thread a small open ring through the last set of large jump rings. Add a small closed jump ring, and then close the open small jump ring.

11. Weave another open small ring through the last attached small jump ring, and add the bar end of the toggle clasp. Close the small jump ring.

:24

►► **Get Set**

Brass sheet, 14 gauge,
 1¾ x 5 inches
 (4.4 x 12.7 cm)

Acrylic sheet, 3 mm,
 1¾ x 4½ inches
 (4.4 x 11.4 cm)

Brass round wire,
 18 gauge, 1 inch
 (2.5 cm)

Bench tool kit, page 9

Acrylic polishing
 compound

Heat gun

Oval bracelet mandrel

FINISHED SIZE
6 x 7 x 4 cm

►►► **Go**

1. Cut out the acrylic and brass sheets to the required size. Mark 10 mm down and 10 mm across from the top right-hand corner of each sheet. Join the markings with a diagonal line, and cut both sheets along this line. Repeat this in the top left-hand corner of each sheet.

2. Sand the sides of the acrylic sheet, working your way up to 1200-grit sand-paper. Polish the sides and surface of the acrylic with a polishing rag and acrylic polishing compound.

3. Anneal the brass sheet, and allow it to cool. File the edges smooth, and create a brushed directional finish on the surface by rubbing it with a coarse scouring pad.

4. Use a heat gun to carefully heat the acrylic until it is flexible. (Heating too much can cause bubbles to form.) Bend the flexible sheet around an oval bracelet mandrel to create a form that fits approximately halfway around the wrist. Hold the acrylic in place on the mandrel until it hardens (approximately 10 seconds). The whole piece, or just certain areas, can be reheated and reshaped if necessary.

5. With a mallet, hammer the brass sheet around the bracelet mandrel so that it fits around the acrylic form. This element forms the other half of the bangle.

6. Place the two pieces together to form a bangle, with the brass piece slightly overlapping the acrylic piece. Stagger them so one piece is higher than the other by about ¼ inch (6 mm). Make sure the diagonal edges of the higher piece are facing up, and the diagonal edges of the lower piece are facing down. If necessary, reheat and reshape the acrylic to ensure a close fit. Tape both pieces together firmly.

7. Using a 1-mm bit, drill two holes through the brass and acrylic sheets at each overlapping section. Prepare to create a hidden rivet by drilling a slight indent over each of the 1-mm holes with a 2-mm bit. Do not go all the way through.

8. Rivet the acrylic and brass pieces together on the bracelet mandrel, spreading the top rivets into the drilled indents of the brass sheet with the hammer. File the rivets flat to create hidden rivets. You may want to reheat the acrylic to remove any stress caused by riveting.

9. Finish by running a scouring pad over the brass sheet to blend the rivets into the brushed finish.

▶ ▶ Get Set

3 natural seed beads,
   each 8 mm

22 natural seed beads,
   each 5 mm

32 natural seed beads,
   each 1 x 3 mm

1 natural seed bead,
   15 mm

Braided leather, brown,
   5½ to 6¾ inches
   (14 to 17.1 cm)

20 brass jump rings,
   20 gauge, each 5 mm

27 brass headpins

Brass curb chain, 3 mm,
   2½ inches (6.4 cm)

2 brass end caps

Brass lobster clasp

Chain-nose pliers

Round-nose pliers

Fabric glue

FINISHED SIZE
26 x 3 x 0.8 cm

DESIGNER'S NOTE
You can use any type of seeds that are dried, polished, and drilled. This bracelet uses three Acai seeds in their natural color, 22 Acai seeds dyed brown, 1 Paxiubinha seed, and 32 Morototó seeds. All these seeds are common to Brazil.

▶ ▶ ▶ Go

1. Select and separate your seed beads.

2. Cut the braided leather to 5½ inches (14 cm) in length.

3. Use needle-nose pliers to attach the 20 brass jump rings along the leather braid, all on the same side.

4. Place the seeds on the headpins as desired, and make a wrapped loop in the top of each headpin with round-nose pliers.

5. Attach one seed bead to each jump ring on the braided leather cord, in an order that pleases you.

6. Use fabric glue to adhere the ends of the braided leather into the end caps. Let the glue dry for 1 hour.

7. Use a jump ring to attach the clasp to one end cap. Use another jump ring to add the curb chain to the other end cap.

8. Attach the remaining beaded headpin to the end of the curb chain.

▶ Get Ready

CUTTING • FILING • SANDING • POLISHING • DIE FORMING

▶▶ Get Set

Patterned copper sheet,
22 gauge, 1½ x 6 inches
(3.8 x 15.2 cm)

Bench shear or scissors

Hydraulic press

Urethane block, at least
95 durometer,
2 inches (5.1 cm) thick,
3 inches (7.6 cm) wide

Anticlastic bracelet-forming
die set

Mini fiber wheel

Bench tool kit, page 9

FINISHED SIZE
3.8 x 6.4 x 5.7 cm

▶▶▶ Go

1. Measure and mark a centerline that divides the copper strip into two 3-inch (7.6 cm) halves. At both ends of the strip, measure and mark points that are 5 mm in from the edges of the metal. With a straight edge, draw a line from the center mark to the 5-mm mark. Repeat for the remaining three corners. Using a bench shear or scissors, cut all four marked lines. File and sand the edges.

2. Polish both sides of the copper to a final finish. Use a mini fiber wheel on the smooth copper side and give the textured side a high polish.

3. Attach a large anticlastic-forming die to a hydraulic press. Center the urethane block on the press plate under the die. Slide the metal under the die, right side down. The end of the metal should extend just past the center of the die, centering the width. Note: The metal should not hang over the outside edge of the die. If the metal is too wide, adjust the width to fall inside the width of the die.

4. Press until you see the metal conform to the shape of the die. Release the pressure slightly so the metal is free. Slide the metal in ½ inch (1.3 cm), and press again. Repeat this process until you reach the end of the metal. Inspect and check for size. You should have an opening of approximately 1 inch (2.5 cm). Re-polish as necessary.

5. To shape the pressed copper into a cuff, replace the large anticlastic die with a smaller anticlastic die. Slide an end of the cuff under the die and just past the center, keeping the cuff width centered. Press just until you see a cuff form. Slide the copper in ½ inch (1.3 cm) and repeat this process. Repeat two times until the end is formed, keeping away from center by 3 inches (7.6 cm). Repeat this step on the other end.

6. Remove and inspect the cuff. It should have a 1-inch (2.5 cm) opening. To customize the cuff, you can make it more round with the large die or close the gap by forming the center of the metal with a smaller die. Re-polish as necessary.

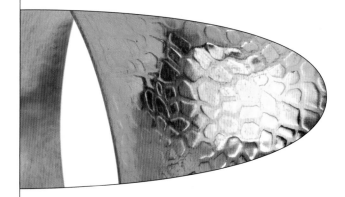

:27

→ ▶ **Get Set**

Fine silver round wire,
10 gauge, 3 inches
(7.6 cm)

Fine silver jump ring,
16 gauge, 8.5 mm

Sterling silver round wire,
12 gauge, 6¾ inches
(17.1 cm)

Scraps of fine silver wire
to use on joints
while fusing

Bench tool kit, page 9

Soldering kit, page 9

FINISHED SIZE
Bracelet, top: 4.4 x 1.9 cm

DESIGNER'S NOTE
Feel free to solder the
piece instead of fusing it if
you are more comfortable
doing so.

▶ ▶ ▶ **Go**

1. File the ends of the 10-gauge fine silver wire, and bend the wire so the ends are flush. Fuse the ends together.

2. Use a rawhide mallet to hammer the fused silver on a ring mandrel to form a circle. Anneal the silver, and then use a large pair of pliers to stretch the circle into an oval shape.

3. On a steel surface, use a cross peen hammer to texture one side of the silver oval. On a ring mandrel, use a planishing hammer to slightly texture the outer edge of the oval, making sure to support the wire so the oval does not lose its shape.

4. Saw the 8.5-mm, 16-gauge fine silver jump ring in half. Use round-nose pliers to form one of the halves into a small jump ring, and fuse the ends together.

5. Place the silver oval on a soldering surface, textured side down. Place the small jump ring on one of the narrow ends of the oval, making sure you have a good fit. Fuse the two pieces together.

6. File the ends of the second 16-gauge fine silver semicircle to fit snugly against the curve on the other narrow end of the oval. Lay the oval on a soldering surface with the hammered texture facing down. Fuse the semicircle in place.

7. Round and smooth the ends of the 12-gauge sterling silver wire with sandpaper or a cup burr.

8. Using round-nose pliers, form a loop on one end of the 12-gauge sterling silver wire. On the other end, form a slight curve up to create a peg. The loop will attach to the half circle on the top bracelet element. The peg will be inserted into the small circle and act as a clasp.

9. Form the bracelet shape around an oval bracelet mandrel. Polish and tumble as desired.

→ Get Ready

SAWING • DRILLING • HAMMERING • FILING • SANDING • RIVETING
BALLING WIRE • USING LIVER OF SULFUR • FINISHING

▶▶ ▶ Get Set

Copper wire, 4 gauge,
8 inches (20.3 cm)

Sterling silver round wire,
18 gauge, 7 inches
(17.8 cm)

Sterling silver round wire,
28 gauge, 2 inches
(5.1 cm)

7 sterling silver headpins,
24 gauge, each ⅝ inch
(1.6 cm)

Sterling silver headpin,
16 gauge, ¾ inch
(1.9 cm)

Bench tool kit, page 9

Torch

FINISHED SIZE
8 x 6.5 x 0.5 cm

DESIGNER'S NOTES
The length of wire used
in this project makes a
medium-sized bangle.

This bangle can be com-
pletely cold connected by
replacing the balled wires
with headpins and riveting.

▶▶ ▶ Go

1. Cut 8 inches (20.3 cm) of 4-gauge
copper wire. Slightly flatten the wire ends with
a flat-faced hammer. File and sand the ends.
Center punch a mark and drill a small starter
hole in the center of each flattened end.

2. Form the copper wire into shape using an
oval bracelet mandrel and a rawhide mallet.
Use your hands to line up the two small
starter holes, and then open the wire ends
and drill each individually with a 16-gauge
drill bit.

3. Line up the drilled holes, and rivet the
wire ends together with the 16-gauge head
pin. Fine-tune the bangle shape with your
hands and the rawhide mallet if necessary.

4. Flatten the side of the bangle opposite
the main rivet with a flat-faced steel hammer.
Use the center punch to make seven divots
on this flat area for the embellishments. Drill
a hole at each divot with a 0.8-mm bit. Using
a center punch or a flat round chasing tool,
add several dots as surface embellishment.

5. Cut the 18-gauge silver wire into seven
pieces, each ¼ to ½ inch (0.6 to 1.3 cm)
long. Flatten each wire end with a ball peen
hammer. File and sand each end.

6. Dimple the center of each flat wire end,
and drill with a 0.5-mm bit. Use flat-nose and
chain-nose pliers to bend each length into a
U shape, matching up the holes.

7. Cut seven pieces of 24-gauge silver wire,
each ¼ inch (6 mm) long. Ball one end of
each wire.

8. One at a time, place each U-shape wire
around the copper wire near the drilled
holes. Align the holes and thread a balled
wire through each U shape and through the
copper wire in the center. Use a torch to ball
the opposite end of each 24-gauge wire,
securing each U in place.

9. Patina the bangle with liver of sulfur. Rub
it lightly with steel wool, and seal it with wax.

29

→ Get Ready

DRILLING • SAWING • BALLING WIRE • WIREWORK • USING JUMP RINGS

→▶ Get Set

6 brass compression
sleeves,
one 1⁵⁄₁₆ inches (3.3 cm),
one 1⅝ inches (4.1 cm),
two 2⅜ inches (6 cm),
and two 2½ inches
(6.4 cm)

Fine silver wire, 18 gauge,
30 inches (76.2 cm)

8 sterling silver jump rings,
16 gauge, ¼-inch
(6 mm) ID (interior
diameter)

Sterling silver lobster clasp

Bench tool kit, page 9

Bench vise

Torch

Tweezers

FINISHED SIZE
20.3 x 1 cm

DESIGNER'S NOTE
Instead of balling the fine
silver wire, you can pur-
chase pre-made 2-inch
(5.1 cm) headpins to use
for the connections.

▶▶▶ Go

1. Line the jaws of a vise with leather to
prevent marring the compression sleeves.
One at a time, clamp each compression
sleeve in a vise and drill two holes opposite
each other using a 1.5-mm bit.

2. Cut the 18-gauge wire into twelve 2½-inch
(6.4 cm) lengths. Use a torch to melt one end
of each wire into a ball.

3. Insert a balled wire through each hole in
each compression sleeve from the inside.
Using round-nose pliers, form a small loop
with no stem in the wire, and spiral the end
of the wire two or three times around the
compression sleeve to form a cap. Repeat
this for all wires.

4. Link the compression sleeves into a
chain with one jump ring in between each
pair. Add a lobster clasp to one end of
the chain and three jump rings to the other
end for adjustability.

DESIGNER: **ELENA BONANOMI**

:30

Get Set

Sterling silver flat wire,
1 x 4 mm, 8½ inches
(22 cm) or more

66 pearl beads,
each 2–2.5 mm

Transparent nylon thread,
0.3 mm, 1 spool

Bench tool kit, page 9

Soldering kit, page 9

FINISHED SIZE
7 x 0.4 x 0.1 cm

Go

1. Determine how much sterling silver flat wire is needed for your desired bracelet size, and cut this amount. For example, 8½ inches (22 cm) makes a small bangle. File and sand the wire to a 400-grit finish.

2. Mark the metal every 2 mm with a permanent marker, and dimple each point.

3. Bend the flat wire into a rough circular shape. File the wire ends flush and solder them together. Pickle and rinse.

4. Place the bracelet on a mandrel, and hammer it with a rawhide mallet to make it perfectly round.

5. Using a 0.6-mm bit, drill a hole at each indentation on the bracelet.

6. Give the bracelet a final finish by brushing it with a brass brush.

7. Cut a 20-inch-long (50.8 cm) nylon thread, and make a double knot at one of the ends.

8. From the outside of the bracelet, thread the nylon through a drilled hole and add a pearl. Thread though the next hole, and add a pearl. Continue until you have gone through each drilled hole. End with a double knot in the last hole.

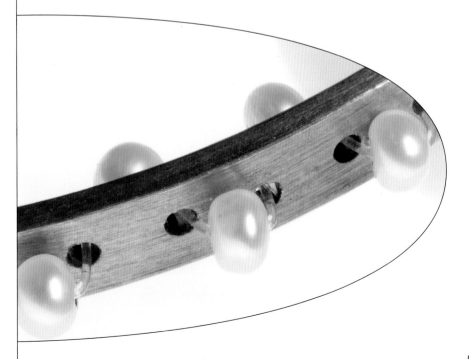

:31

➤ Get Ready

USING A DISK CUTTER • DRILLING • SANDING • HAMMERING • TEXTURING
DOMING • BALLING WIRE • SOLDERING • WIREWORK • POLISHING

➤➤ ▶ Get Set

Sterling silver round wire,
16 gauge, 4¼ inches
(11.4 cm)

12 sterling silver jump
rings, 18 gauge,
each 5 mm

Sterling silver sheet,
22 gauge,
2½ x 2 inches
(6.4 x 5.1 cm)

Bench tool kit, page 9

Soldering kit, page 9

FINISHED SIZE
18.4 x 1.9 cm

➤➤ ▶ Go

1. Use a disk cutter to cut four ¾-inch (1.9 cm) circles and five ⅜-inch (0.95 cm) circles from the 22-gauge silver sheet.

2. Draw a centerline across each silver circle with a permanent marker. Make two marks on the centerline of each circle, each 2 mm inside the edge of the metal. Center punch and drill these points using a 1.3-mm bit.

3. Randomly drill holes and use a disk cutter to create holes in each silver circle to create a pattern. Sand each silver circle to a 240-grit finish.

4. Place each silver circle on a steel block and texture it with a planishing hammer.

5. Gently dome each circle in a dapping block, using a low depression.

6. Make the toggle bar by cutting 2 inches (5.1 cm) of 16-gauge round wire. Use round-nose pliers to form a loop in the center of the wire. Ball the ends of the wire with a torch. Solder the loop in the center where the wire crosses.

7. Make the toggle ring by wrapping 16-gauge wire around a ¾-inch (1.9 cm) mandrel. Cut the ring, arrange the wires flush, and solder together.

8. Join the silver circle links through the holes drilled in step 2 using 5-mm, 18-gauge jump rings. Alternate large and small circles as you make the chain.

9. Attach a jump ring to the toggle ring and one to the toggle bar. Attach the toggle ends to the bracelet.

10. Solder the jump rings closed. File the seams and hammer texture the jump rings and the toggle on a steel block. Polish the bracelet using a tumbler with steel shot.

:32

SAWING • FILING • ANNEALING • FORMING
BRAIDING • SOLDERING • FINISHING

▶ ▶ **Get Set**

Sterling silver round wire,
    14 gauge, 17.7 inches
    (45 cm)

Bench tool kit, page 9

Soldering kit, page 9

Bench vise

FINISHED SIZE
6.4 x 4.4 x 1.9 cm

▶ ▶ ▶ **Go**

1. Determine the length of the sterling silver wire needed for your desired bracelet size. Add 1 to 1½ inches (2.5 to 3.8 cm) to this length. Measure and cut three wires of this size. File the wire ends flat, and anneal if needed.

2. Gently flatten the three wires with a mallet. Using a permanent marker or scribe, determine and mark the center of the wires. Mark 1 to 1½ inches (2.5 to 3.8 cm) away from the centerline on both sides, indicating where you will begin and end braiding the wire. Taping the wires together may help you with this step.

3. Place the wires into a vise at one of the lines marked in the previous step. Braid the wire as you would braid hair. Use a thin dowel to keep the loops even. Stop braiding when you arrive at the other marked point. Try to have all three ends meet before taking the wires out of the vise.

4. Cut two 2½-inch (6.4 cm) pieces of 14-gauge wire. Anneal if needed. Wrap one wire around each end of the braid twice, and cut excess wire from the back of the loops. File and sand.

5. From the back of the bracelet, solder the looped wires onto the braided wire. Pickle and clean.

6. To achieve your desired bracelet size, measure equal distances from the looped wires to the end of the wires on both ends. Cut the wires, and file flat. Solder the wires together near the ends. Pickle and clean. File the ends round, removing any roughness.

7. Form the cuff around an oval bracelet mandrel at your desired size. Give the cuff a final finish by brushing it with a brass brush or rubbing it with steel wool.

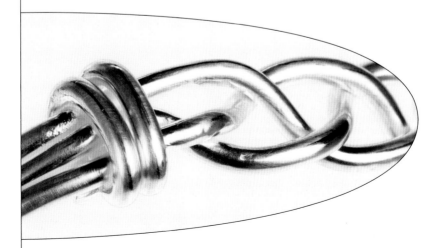

:33

▶ Get Ready

**SOLDERING • WIREWORK • SAWING
BALLING WIRE • HAMMERING • FINISHING**

▶▶ ▶ Get Set

Sterling silver round wire,
18 gauge, 19 inches
(48.3 cm)

7 sterling silver jump rings,
18 gauge, each 4 mm

Sterling silver jump ring,
18 gauge, 6 mm

Bench tool kit, page 9

Soldering kit, page 9

FINISHED SIZE
20 x 0.7 cm

▶▶ ▶ Go

1. Close and solder the jump rings.

2. With needle-nose pliers, carefully stretch the 4-mm jump rings into ovals.

3. Cut the sterling silver wire into eight pieces, each measuring 2½ inches (6.4 cm).

4. Ball both ends of each piece of wire, holding it at a 45-degree angle to the torch flame so the balls form slightly off center.

5. Hold one piece of balled wire a quarter of the way down its length. With needle-nose pliers, bend the smaller end toward the middle of the wire, forming a teardrop shape. Make sure the balled end is angled out. Reposition the pliers on the tail end of the wire. Bend the wire toward the middle, forming the scroll shape. Repeat this step to shape the remaining seven balled-wire pieces.

6. With a planishing hammer and a steel block, lightly planish both ends of each scroll, flattening and hardening the wires.

7. Assemble the bracelet by threading each small jump ring through one side of two scrolls. Begin the bracelet with the large jump ring. End the bracelet with a scroll shape that will function as the clasp.

8. Solder the balled ends of the scrolls to the middle of the wire. On the last scroll, only solder one of the balled ends so the other will act as the hook of the clasp.

9. Tumble the bracelet in steel shot to work harden and burnish the metal.

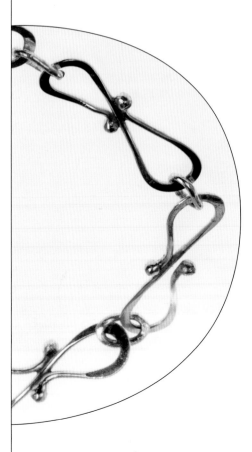

DESIGNER: **ANN L. LUMSDEN**

:34

► ► **Get Set**

Sterling silver rectangular
wire, 2 x 4 mm,
8¼ inches (21 cm)

16 sterling silver ear
posts with pads,
each 0.78 mm

16 round dyed jade beads,
each 6 mm

Bench tool kit, page 9

Soldering kit, page 9

Hammer hand piece

Dividers

FINISHED SIZE
7.5 x 0.5 cm

DESIGNER'S NOTE
Jade is a very tough stone
and usually withstands the
pressure of riveting, but
occasionally a bead will
crack, so have a few extras
on hand.

► ► ► **Go**

1. Bend the rectangular sterling silver wire
into a rough circle, making sure the two ends
line up closely.

2. Solder the wire ends together. Pickle the
silver form, and clean up the solder joint with
files and sandpaper.

3. Use a mallet to round the bangle
on a bracelet mandrel. Sand and polish
the bangle.

4. Using dividers, mark 16 equidistant
and centered points around the bangle.
Drill holes at the marked points using a
0.8-mm bit.

5. Support the bangle on a steel bracelet
mandrel. Lightly hammer the entire outside
surface with the ball end of a hammer,
avoiding the drill holes.

6. Re-drill any of the holes that became
distorted during hammering. Use a ball burr
on the inside of the bangle to countersink the
holes. Lightly repolish the top and sides of
the bangle.

7. Sand and polish the flat pad end of the
ear posts. Thread one through a bead, and
then onto the bangle. Cut off the end of
the post wire, leaving approximately 1 mm
exposed inside the bangle. Support the post
and bead on a steel block. Rivet the exposed
wire inside the bangle with a hammer hand
piece so the wire spreads out to fill the
countersunk hole. Repeat this process until
all the beads are riveted in place.

8. File, sand, and polish the inside of the
bangle. Carefully polish the top and sides,
and clean the finished piece.

:35

▶ Get Ready

SAWING • FILING • BENDING • SOLDERING HAMMERING • POLISHING • KNOTTING

▶▶ ▶ Get Set

Sterling silver round wire, 16 gauge, 27 inches (68.6 cm)

3 beads with large holes, each ½ inch (1.3 cm)

Embroidery floss, hemp, or linen twine, several colors, each 24 inches (61 cm)

Cyanoacrylite glue

Bench tool kit, page 9

Soldering kit, page 9

FINISHED SIZE
7.6 x 7.6 cm

▶▶ ▶ Go

1. Cut the 16-gauge silver wire into three pieces, each measuring 9 inches (22.9 cm). File the ends flat. Bend the wire lengths into round bangle shapes, meeting the ends together. Place one bead on each bangle, and position the bead opposite the wire ends. Solder the wire ends.

2. One at a time, place each bangle on a bench block and hammer both sides flat. Polish the hammered bangles with steel wool.

3. Using the thread of your choice, tie a square knot around one bangle just above the solder joint, leaving a 3-inch (7.6 cm) tail on one side. Holding the tail against the bangle, make a series of half-hitch knots that cover the tail and the bangle. The knots naturally want to spiral around the bangle, so they may need to be straightened. Once you complete ½ inch (1.3 cm) of half-hitch knots, string the thread through the bead and continue knotting for another ½ inch (1.3 cm).

4. Tie a square knot with the tail and remaining thread. Dot the knot with a drop of glue. If you're using a plied thread, such as embroidery floss, separate the individual strands of thread.

5. Repeat steps 3 and 4 for each bangle.

DESIGNER: **AMY PROFF LYONS**

:36

▶ Get Ready

**ANNEALING • ROLLER PRINTING (OPTIONAL) • APPLYING A HAMMER TEXTURE
FORMING • FILING • FINISHING • USING LIVER OF SULFUR**

▶ ▶ Get Set

Brass sheet, 18 gauge,
    1 x 6 inches
    (2.5 x 15.2 cm)

Copper sheet, 24 gauge,
    ½ x 6 inches
    (1.3 x 15.2 cm)

Sterling silver wire,
    14 gauge, 6 inches
    (15.2 cm)

Bench tool kit, page 9

Soldering kit, page 9

Chasing tools

FINISHED SIZE
2.5 x 15.2 cm

▶ ▶ ▶ Go

1. Anneal the brass and copper strips. Pickle and clean the metal. Roller print the metal or hammer it with a texturing hammer.

2. Place the copper strip on the brass strip, and trace it with a permanent marker. Apply flux to the brass strip only where the copper will be attached. Apply flux to the entire back of the copper strip. Cut small pieces of solder, and melt them to the back of the copper. Flip the copper over, and solder it to the brass strip. Pickle and rinse.

3. Place the sterling silver wire on top of the copper. Trace around it with a permanent marker. Apply flux to the copper only where the silver wire will be attached. Apply flux to the silver wire, and melt solder to the wire. Solder the silver wire to the copper. Pickle and rinse.

4. Add texture to the sterling silver with chasing tools and a hammer. Shape the metal around a bracelet mandrel with a rawhide mallet.

5. Use a needle file to file the edges of the cuff. Use a fine pumice wheel in a flexible shaft to smooth the edges.

6. Oxidize the cuff with liver of sulfur, and use pumice powder to take off the oxidation you do not want.

7. Leave the cuff with a matte finish, or tumble it with steel shot for a shiny finish.

DESIGNER: **THERESA ST. ROMAIN**

→ Get Ready

CUTTING · FILING · BENDING · SOLDERING · SANDING · FINISHING

►► Get Set

Brass sheet, 18 gauge,
9 x ¾ inch
(22.8 x 1.8 cm)

Bench tool kit, page 9

Soldering kit, page 9

Bench polisher with bristle
wheels, 80 and 120 grit

FINISHED SIZE
10.2 x 0.6 x 1.9 cm

►►► Go

1. Cut the brass sheet into two pieces, one 5 inches (12.7 cm) and the other 4 inches (10.2 cm). File the corners on one end of each piece round.

2. Using your fingers, gently curve each brass sheet.

3. File a beveled edge on the ends of the brass sheets that were not rounded in step 1. The beveled ends will be soldered together and should be flush to each other.

4. Stand the brass pieces vertically on their long edges with the two beveled edges together, and solder. File and sand as needed.

5. Using your fingers, curve the bracelet as needed to acheive the final form.

6. Use the bristle wheels on the bench polisher to get a final matte finish.

Have time to spare?

As shown in the detail, add a green patina to create a different look.

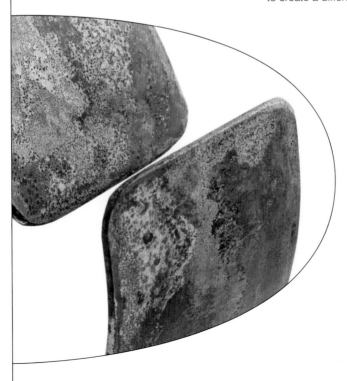

:38

▶▶ ▶ Get Set

Black steel wire, 16 gauge,
1 spool

32 gold-plated closed jump
rings, each 4 mm

Gold-plated toggle clasp

3 mandrels: 3.5 mm,
4.5 mm, and 8.5 mm

Jeweler's saw

2 pairs of chain-nose pliers

FINISHED SIZE
0.6 x 19 cm

▶ ▶ ▶ Go

1. Make jump rings from the black steel wire in these measurements: eight 11.5-mm rings, nine 7.5-mm rings, and two 6.5-mm rings.

2. Make a 1-inch (2.5 cm) steel jump ring, and thread some of the gold-plated jump rings onto it. Use pliers to flatten the gold rings into an oval shape that will accommodate two steel rings. (The solder joints on these gold-plated rings occasionally crack when you stretch them, so have a few spares on hand.)

3. Link the steel jump rings using two of the oval gold ones and alternating between large and medium-sized steel rings. Tip: The black coating on the steel wire mars easily, so use nylon-jawed pliers or wrap the jaws of steel pliers in tape when opening and closing the jump rings.

4. Use the two smallest steel jump rings to attach the two toggle components and complete the bracelet.

:39

> **Get Ready**

SAWING • FILING • SANDING • FORMING • SOLDERING
DRILLING • FINISHING • SEWING

►► Get Set

Sterling silver flat wire,
  1 x 4 mm, 8½ inches
  (22 cm)

Waxed blue thread,
  1 mm, 1 spool

Bench tool kit, page 9

Soldering kit, page 9

FINISHED SIZE
7 x 0.4 x 0.1 cm

►►► Go

1. Determine how much sterling silver flat wire you need for the desired bracelet size, and cut this length. A small bangle is approximately 8½ inches (22 cm) of wire. File and sand the wire to a 400-grit finish.

2. Choose the desired stitch pattern, and mark it on the metal with a permanent marker. For a regular pattern, make marks at even intervals, such as every 2 mm. For an irregular pattern, mark the metal at different distances, such as 4 mm then 2 mm then 4 mm then 2 mm. Dimple each marked point.

3. Bend the flat wire into a rough circular shape, and then file the ends flush. Solder, pickle, and rinse the bracelet.

4. Place the bracelet on a mandrel, and hammer it with a rawhide mallet to make it perfectly round.

5. Using a 0.6-mm bit, drill a hole at each indentation on the bracelet.

6. Give the bracelet a final finish by brushing it with a brass brush.

7. Cut a 20-inch (50.8 cm) length of waxed blue thread, and make a double knot at one of the ends.

8. Thread the waxed blue thread through the drilled holes. End with a double knot in the last hole.

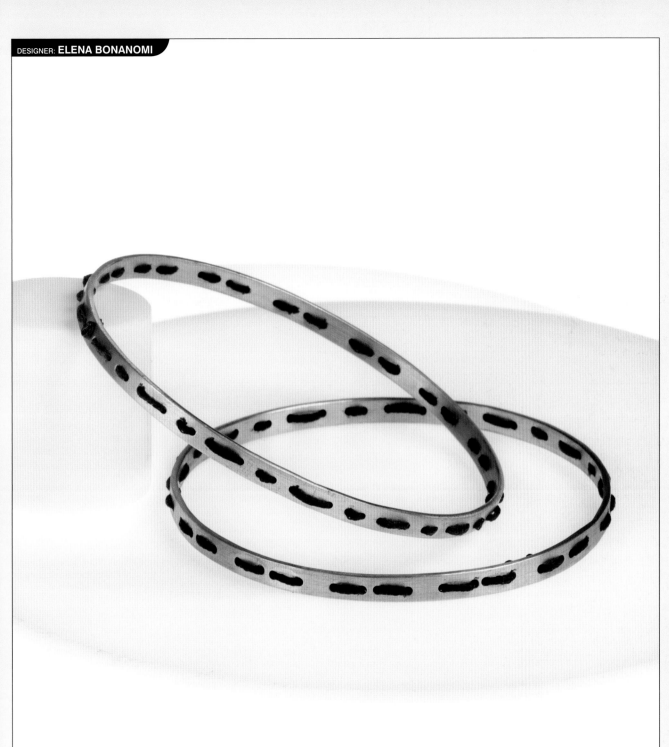

:40

▶ **Get Ready**

FILING · SANDING · SOLDERING · FORMING · ROLLER PRINTING
DRILLING · USING A DISK CUTTER · DAPPING · BALLING WIRE · FINISHING

▶ ▶ **Get Set**

Copper round wire,
10 gauge, 7¾ inches
(19.7 cm)

Patterned brass sheet,
24 gauge, 1 x 2 inches
(2.5 x 5.1 cm)

Copper round wire,
20 gauge, 6¼ inches
(15.9 cm)

Bench tool kit, page 9

Soldering kit, page 9

FINISHED SIZE
8.3 x 5.7 x 0.6 cm

▶ ▶ ▶ **Go**

1. File the ends of the 10-gauge copper wire flat, and solder them together. Use a rawhide mallet to hammer the bracelet into shape on an oval bracelet mandrel. Level the bangle with a rawhide mallet on a steel block.

2. Flatten the bangle by rolling it through a rolling mill until it is 1.4 mm thick.

3. Drill nine 0.6-mm holes on the horizontal plane of the bangle. Group six holes on one side and three on the other, and separate the holes by approximately ⅜ inch (1 cm). File and sand the bangle.

4. Use a circle template to trace nine ⁵⁄₁₆-inch (8 mm) circles on the patterned brass sheet. Drill a 0.6-mm hole in the center of each circle.

5. Use a disk cutter to punch out the nine traced circles. Take care to line up the traced circle in the cutter to keep the drilled hole in the center of each brass disk.

6. Using a dapping block and an appropriate dap, dome each brass disk with the pattern on the inside of the dome. File or sand any rough or sharp edges.

7. Cut the 20-gauge copper wire into five pieces, each 1¼ inches (3.2 cm) long. Ball both ends of each wire, and cut the wires in half.

8. Place a balled wire into each dome, cup side up, and then into every other hole on the flat bangle. Trim the wires, leaving 4 mm sticking out under the bangle. One at a time, ball these wires with a torch.

9. Repeat step 8 for the remaining cups and wires, installing them in the empty holes on the reverse side of the flat bangle. Pickle the bracelet.

10. Give the bangle a final finish by tumbling it with steel shot or using liver of sulfur and a green scrub pad.

→► **Get Set**

Two-part molding
compound

Sterling silver metal clay,
20 grams

Sterling silver round wire,
18 gauge, 1½ inches
(3.8 cm)

Sterling silver round wire,
16 gauge, 10 inches
(25.4 cm)

Wire mesh for drying

Oven or dehydrator

Kiln preheated to 1472°F
(800°C)

Round mandrels,
10 mm, 6 mm, and
2 mm in diameter

Dried poppy head

Bench tool kit, page 9

Soldering kit, page 9

FINISHED SIZE
1.9 x 16.5 cm

DESIGNER'S NOTE
Add a cubic zirconia to the
center of the poppy head
for a little sparkle.

►►► **Go**

1. Mix equal amounts of the blue and the
white molding compound until the color is
uniform with no marbling. Make a mold of the
poppy head, and allow it to set. Remove the
mold from the poppy.

2. Remove the clay from its package, and
pinch off one fifth of the clay. Form it into a
ball and push it into the mold. Release the
clay from the mold, and set it on the mesh to
dry. Repeat this process until you have five
poppy heads. Dry in an oven or dehydrator
for 10 minutes.

3. While the clay dries, wrap the 16-gauge
sterling silver wire completely around a
10-mm mandrel six times. Remove the coil
from the mandrel, and saw through the rings
with a jeweler's saw.

4. Use round-nose pliers to form the
18-gauge silver wire into 12 C shapes,
each about 6 mm long and 4 mm wide.
Snip the wire with flush cutters, and file the
bottoms flush.

5. Sand the back of each clay poppy head
flat. Place them into the preheated kiln and
fire for 5 minutes.

6. Cut a length of 16-gauge sterling wire,
approximately 1 inch (2.5 cm) long. File and
round the ends. Cut a shorter length of wire,
and form it into a C shape about 8 mm long
and 6 mm wide. Sand the ends flush, and
solder it to the 1-inch (2.5 cm) wire, forming
a toggle.

7. Wrap the 18-gauge wire around the 2-mm
mandrel, and cut one jump ring. Attach it to
the toggle, and solder it closed. Wrap the
18-gauge wire around the 5-mm mandrel,
and cut two jump rings. Attach one of them
to the small jump ring, and solder closed.

8. Remove the poppy heads from the kiln
and quench. Solder two C-shaped pieces
made in step 4 to the back of each poppy,
at opposite edges (see detail).

9. Attach the metal flowers together with the
10-mm jump rings, and solder each closed.
Attach the toggle to the last C with the
remaining jump ring, and solder it closed.

10. Pickle, rinse, and brush the bracelet
with a brass brush.

Have time to spare?

Tumble your bracelet for a high shine or add
a patina for extra depth.

:42

▶▶ ▶ Get Set

Sterling silver or brass
    sheet, 18 gauge,
    6 x 3 inches
    (15.2 x 7.6 cm)

Sterling silver or brass
    wire, 14 gauge, 3 inches
    (7.6 cm)

Sterling silver or brass
    wire, 20 to 22 gauge
    depending on your
    beads, 2 feet (61 cm)

Large, drilled gemstone
    beads of your choice

Bench tool kit, page 9

Soldering kit, page 9

FINISHED SIZE
15.2 x 7.6 cm

DESIGNER'S NOTE
Save time by purchasing
a pre-made cuff from a
jewelry supplier.

▶▶ ▶ Go

1. Round the corners of the sheet metal with a file, and then use 220- and 400-grit sandpaper to smooth the edges. If you would like a hammered finish, as shown in the project photo, use a ball-peen hammer to texture the sheet. Form the sheet metal around an oval bracelet mandrel with a rawhide or wooden mallet.

2. Use chain-nose pliers to gently curve the 14-gauge wire into a shallow arc that is nearly as long as the cuff is wide. File the ends of the wire flat, and check the fit against the cuff bracelet.

3. Solder the wire arc vertically onto the center of the cuff. Pickle, rinse, and dry.

4. Polish the bracelet to the desired finish.

5. Cut the thin wire into at least six 3-inch (7.6 cm) lengths. Ball the end of each wire with a torch. Pickle, rinse, and dry.

6. Thread a bead onto a balled wire. Make a loop at the end of the wire, and loop it through the wire on the cuff. Tightly bring the wire tail back around the wire at the base of the bead, and wrap twice to form a short coil. Snip off any extra wire length. Tightly pinch the end of the wire against the coil with chain-nose pliers.

7. Repeat step 6 until the arc is covered with beads to your liking.

VARIATION

:43

➤ Get Ready

FORMING · FILING · SOLDERING · POLISHING · GLUING

▶▶ ▶ Get Set

Sterling silver square wire,
10 gauge, 19¼ inches
(48.9 cm)

Sterling silver round wire,
18 gauge, 10 mm

2 half-drilled pearls,
each 8 mm

Bench tool kit, page 9

Soldering kit, page 9

FINISHED SIZE
7.6 x 7 cm

▶▶ ▶ Go

1. Bend the sterling silver square wire around an oval bracelet mandrel. Start on the front of the mandrel, and completely wrap the silver around it twice.

2. File the square wire ends flat.

3. Snip the 18-gauge round wire into two 5-mm pieces. Solder one wire to each end of the coil perpendicularly and in the center of the flat surface. These are the posts for the pearls.

4. Polish the bracelet. Adhere the pearls to the posts with epoxy.

Want to make another bracelet?

As shown in the variation, use 10-gauge round wire, only wrap the it around the mandrel once, and feature a different pearl color.

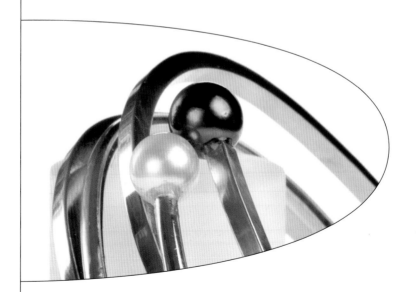

DESIGNER: **SUSAN MACHAMER**

:44

Get Ready

SAWING • FILING • FORMING • SOLDERING
FORGING • SANDING • POLISHING

Get Set

Sterling silver round wire, 8 gauge, 6½ inches (16.5 cm)

Bench tool kit, page 9

Soldering kit, page 9

FINISHED SIZE
6.4 x 6.4 x 0.4 cm

DESIGNER'S NOTE
The length of silver suggested for this bracelet makes a small size bangle.

Go

1. Cut a 6½-inch (16.5 cm) length of 8-gauge sterling silver wire. File both ends completely flat, and solder them together.

2. Shape the soldered bangle on a round bracelet mandrel with a rawhide mallet. Use a circle template to mark eight equal points around the bangle.

3. Place the bangle on an anvil and begin forging four opposite sections with a planishing hammer. Begin hammering in the center of two marks and gradually hammer up to the marks made in step 2. Take care to create a nice, smooth taper with the widest part in the center of two marks. Work slowly and use intentional hammer blows.

4. Place the bangle on the round bracelet mandrel. Forge the four remaining sections using the same technique described in step 3. When finished, the bangle should be round on the inside and square on the outside.

5. Shape the bangle with a rawhide mallet on an anvil and on a bracelet mandrel to ensure that it is formed evenly.

6. Sand the bangle to a 600-grit finish. Polish it to a rouge shine.

:45

➤ ➤ ➤ **Get Set**

Sterling silver flat wire,
4 x 1 mm, 21 inches
(47.6 cm)

Sterling silver flat wire,
2 x 1 mm, 2 inches
(5.1 cm)

Steel round wire,
20 gauge, 24 inches
(50.8 cm)

3 aluminum sheets,
20 gauge, 7 x 1 inches
(17.8 x 2.5 cm)

Coarse sandpaper,
50 to 150 grit

Bench tool kit, page 9

Soldering kit, page 9

FINISHED SIZE
6 x 1 x 0.2 cm

➤ ➤ ➤ **Go**

1. Use a saw to cut three lengths of the 4 x 1-mm flat wire, each 7 inches (17.8 cm). Anneal the wires.

2. Sandwich the three wire lengths cut in step 1 between the coarse sandpapers. Roller print the sandpaper pattern into the wires.

3. Sandwich the three textured wires between the aluminum sheets. Arrange the steel wires as a design source inside the aluminum sheets, and roller print.

4. Cut each wire length 7 inches (17.8 cm) long, and file the ends flush. Bend the ends of each wire around to meet, and solder. Pickle, rinse, and dry the bangles.

5. Place each bangle on a round bracelet mandrel, and hammer with a rawhide mallet.

6. Score and bend the 2-inch (5.1 cm) silver flat wire into a rectangle. Solder the three bent joints, leaving the last joint open. Pickle, rinse, and dry.

7. Insert the three bangles into the silver rectangle through the open joint. Align the joint so the pieces are touching, and solder it together. Pickle, rise and dry.

8. File and sand the joint soldered in step 7. Gently rub the bangles with fine-grit steel wool for a final finish.

:46

▶▶ ▶ **Get Set**

Sterling silver round wire,
    16 gauge, 17¾ inches
    (45.1 cm)

10 sterling silver jump
    rings, 18 gauge,
    each 5 mm

6 glass beads, each 8 mm

Bench tool kit, page 9

Soldering kit, page 9

FINISHED SIZE
19.75 x 1.3 cm

▶▶ ▶ **Go**

1. Fully wrap the 16-gauge silver wire around a ¾-inch (1.9 cm) dowel six times. Cut apart the individual rings. Thread a glass bead onto each ring, and close it.

2. Solder each ring, focusing the heat on the joint and away from the glass bead. Let each ring air cool before pickling.

3. Using round-nose pliers, shape each ring into a teardrop. Pinch one end with needle-nose pliers to make the small end of each silver teardrop shape.

4. Texture each silver teardrop on a steel block with a planishing hammer. Be careful not to crack the glass beads.

5. To make the toggle bar, cut 2 inches (5.1 cm) of 16-gauge round wire. Use round-nose pliers to make a loop in the center of the wire. Ball the ends of the wire with a torch. Solder the loop in the center where the wire crosses.

6. Make the toggle ring by wrapping 16-gauge wire around a ¾-inch (1.9 cm) mandrel. Cut the ring, arrange the wires flush, and solder.

7. Attach one 5-mm jump ring to each silver teardrop. As you attach a jump ring to each link, alternate the placement of the glass beads from one side to the other.

8. Attach an additional jump ring to the toggle ring and two additional jump rings to the toggle bar. Attach the toggle ends to the teardrop links to complete the bracelet. Adjust the length of the bracelet by widening or narrowing the teardrop links with round-nose pliers.

9. Solder the jump rings and let them air cool. File the seams, and then hammer-texture the jump rings and the toggle on a steel block.

10. Polish the bracelet using a tumbler and steel shot.

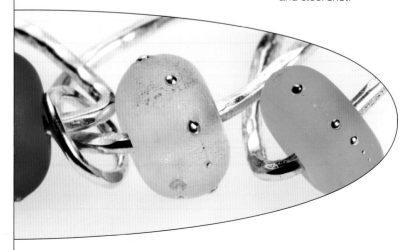

DESIGNER: **DEBORAH E. LOVE JEMMOTT**

Get Ready

FORMING · FILING · DRILLING · SOLDERING · FINISHING

▶▶ Get Set

Copper round wire,
12 gauge, 9 inches
(22.9 cm)

Decorative "spanner"
element, 3½ inches
(8.8 cm)

Bench tool kit, page 9

Soldering kit, page 9

Metal dish, 2 to 3 inches
(5.1 to 7.6 cm) deep,
filled with water
almost to the top

FINISHED SIZE
7 x 8.9 cm

DESIGNER'S NOTE
The "spanner" element can
be any material that can be
submerged in water without
damage and can have
holes drilled or punched
into it.

▶▶▶ Go

1. Form the copper wire into a circle with your fingers. File the ends flush. Hammer the wire round on a mandrel, making sure the ends meet.

2. Mark the decorative "spanner" element where the holes need to be drilled. The holes should be 2¼ inches (5.7 cm) apart, centered on the element horizontally and vertically. Drill the holes with a 3-mm bit. Using the same bit, go back through the drilled holes to create an angle on the interior side of each hole to accommodate the curved wire.

3. Thread the decorative element onto the wire, taking care not to distort the wire.

4. Submerge the decorative element into the water-filled metal bowl. Hold the bracelet in place with self-locking tweezers, making sure the tweezers are low on the bracelet near the water. The solder joint should be at the highest point, away from the water.

5. Use easy solder to solder the bracelet together. Point the torch flame up from the inside of the bracelet or across the bracelet parallel with the surface of the water. Do not point the flame toward the decorative element or toward the water.

6. File and sand the solder joint, and give the metal a final finish.

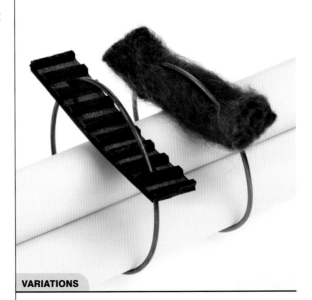

VARIATIONS

:48

▶▶ ▶ Get Set

Sterling silver round wire, 16 gauge, 18 inches (45.7 cm)

Sterling silver round wire, 20 gauge, 7.5 inches (19.1 cm)

Four sterling silver jump rings, 16 gauge, 8 mm OD (outside diameter)

Five flat oval stone beads, each 10 x 14 mm

Bench tool kit, page 9

Soldering kit, page 9

Liver of sulfur

FINISHED SIZE
16.5 x 1.9 cm

DESIGNER'S NOTE
Snowflake obsidian works well as it does not heat crack easily and is pickle safe.

▶ ▶ ▶ Go

1. Cut ten 1½-inch (3.8 cm) pieces of 16-gauge wire, and file the wire ends flat. You should have a 3-inch (7.6 cm) piece leftover; set it aside for later use.

2. With a planishing hammer on a steel bench block, forge both ends of the wire flat and wide enough to accommodate a 20-gauge drill hole. Center punch about 2 mm from each wire end, and drill a hole with a 0.8-mm bit. File off any burrs.

3. Bend each wire over a mandrel into a U shape. The curve should be about as wide as your bead, and the drill holes should line up with the hole in the bead. Adjust the wire with pliers if needed. Gently flatten the curved area of each U-shaped wire with a planishing hammer on a bench block.

4. Cut five 1½-inch (3.8 cm) pieces of 20-gauge wire. Use a torch to ball one end of each piece of wire. Pickle, rinse, and set aside.

5. Take the 3-inch (7.6 cm) piece of 16-gauge wire set aside earlier, and bend it in half. Planish the wire flat, and form it into a hook-shaped clasp. Solder it closed. Also solder closed the four jump rings. Pickle and rinse.

6. Assemble your bracelet, and ball the unfinished ends of the five 20-gauge wires. Do not quench. After the piece has cooled, pickle, rinse, and scratch brush it.

7. Finish the bracelet with liver of sulfur, and polish it with a green scrub pad to remove some of the oxidization.

:49

▶ Get Ready

SAWING • **FILING** • **SANDING** • **HAMMERING** • **SOLDERING**
WIREWORK • **POLISHING** • **STRINGING**

▶▶ Get Set

Sterling silver sheet,
   20 gauge, 1 x 1½ inches
   (2.5 x 4 cm)

Sterling silver round wire,
   18 gauge, 2½ inches
   (6 cm)

2 sterling silver
   crimp beads

16 faceted beads,
   each 10 mm

Closed jump ring, 4 mm

Bench tool kit, page 9

Soldering kit, page 9

Binding wire

Beading cable

Photocopied design
   template ❶

FINISHED SIZE
20 cm

▶▶▶ Go

1. Transfer the oak leaf template onto the silver sheet. Saw out the leaf shape. Use needle files to smooth and refine the shape. Sand both sides of the leaf to a 400-grit finish.

2. Cut a piece of binding wire long enough to fit down the center of the silver leaf. You'll use this wire to create the center leaf vein. Cut four more pieces of binding wire to use for the shorter leaf veins.

3. Cut a length of tape longer than the leaf, and use this to affix the longest piece of wire to the leaf. Gently hammer the wire into the sheet, carefully lifting the tape to check your progress. The tape will protect the rest of the leaf from the hammer.

4. Repeat the process described in step 3 with each of the four shorter wires, taping them and hammering them one at a time.

5. Cut a 2¼-inch (5.7 cm) length of 18-gauge wire, and make a loop at one end with round-nose pliers. Use a small hammer to slightly flatten a ¾-inch (1.9 cm) wire section next to the loop. This makes soldering easier.

6. Place the silver leaf face down on a soldering block. Use a third hand and cross-locking tweezers to hold the wire along the center of the leaf with the loop behind the stem. Solder the wire in place. Pickle, rinse, and dry.

7. Use a needle file or cup burr to smooth the end of the wire. Use chain-nose pliers to bend the wire back on itself to form a hook, and bend up the last 5 mm of wire to make the hook easier to fasten. Polish the clasp to a rouge shine.

8. Cut 10 inches (25.4 cm) of beading cable. Thread a crimp bead and the jump ring on the cable, and then thread it back through the crimp bead to form a small loop at one end of the cable. Close the crimp bead.

9. Thread the faceted beads onto the cable to make the desired bracelet length, taking the length of the clasp into account. Thread a crimp bead onto the cable, and push the cable back down through to form a small loop. Hide the excess cable inside the beads, and close the crimp.

10. Attach the clasp to the bracelet using the loop in the wire hook.

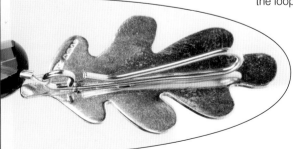

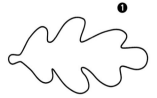

❶

:50

▶ Get Ready

WIREWORK · ANNEALING · FORGING · SOLDERING

▶ ▶ Get Set

Copper wire, 14 gauge,
   35½ inches (90 cm)

Bench tool kit, page 9

Soldering kit, page 9

Photocopied design
   template ❶
   enlarge 200%

FINISHED SIZE
6.4 x 3.8 cm

▶ ▶ ▶ Go

1. Use snips to cut two 17¾-inch (45 cm) lengths of 14-gauge copper wire.

2. Use your fingers to bend each wire into seven "doodle loops" as shown in the template. Leave a 1-inch (2.5 cm) tail on one of the wires. Anneal.

3. Open each wire loop to a 90-degree angle. Hammer each side of the wire with a flat-faced hammer, and then close each hammered loop. Anneal.

4. Adjust each wire segment by squeezing and stretching it with your fingers to produce a 6⅓-inch (16 cm) length and a 6⅔-inch (17 cm) length, not counting the tail.

5. Place the shorter wire segment on top of the longer wire segment, and solder the end loops together. Pickle, rinse, and dry.

6. Bend the bracelet around an oval mandrel, and hammer the wires with a rawhide mallet to work harden them.

7. Using round-nose pliers, bend the wire tail back toward the bracelet, reposition the pliers, and then bend the tail away from the bracelet to form an S shape. Snip the end of the wire to a 3-mm length, round it with a file, and close the S with flat nose pliers.

Want to make another bracelet?

Make a single layer cuff with 12- or 10-gauge wire.

Make a triple layer bracelet with copper, silver, and brass.

❶

51

→ Get Ready

SAWING • FILING • SOLDERING • FORMING • WRAPPING YARN

▶▶ ▶ Get Set

Steel binding wire,
   14 gauge, 7 inches
   (17.8 cm)

Cotton yarn in color
   of your choice

Bench tool kit, page 9

Soldering kit, page 9

FINISHED SIZE
22 x 7.6 x 0.64 cm

▶ ▶ ▶ Go

1. Determine the length of steel wire needed for your desired bracelet size. Mark and cut the metal at this point. File the ends of the wire flat, and solder them together.

2. Place the soldered wire on a bracelet mandrel, and hammer it with a rawhide mallet. Clean the bracelet with soap and water to remove any grease. Dry completely.

3. Cut a length of cotton yarn, approximately 12 feet (3.65 m) long. Tie one end of the yarn securely around the bracelet.

4. Begin wrapping the yarn around the bracelet, keeping each wrap close to the preceding one and covering the steel completely. As you wrap, you can wind the yarn over and over in certain areas to create bumps. Continue wrapping until the entire bracelet is covered. Add more yarn as needed. Secure the end of the yarn, and clip.

52

➤ Get Ready

SAWING · FILING · ANNEALING · FORMING
FORGING · SOLDERING · FINISHING

➤➤ Get Set

Sterling silver round wire,
10 gauge, 11½ inches
(29.2 cm) for a small
to medium cuff

Oval bracelet mandrel

Bench tool kit, page 9

Soldering kit, page 9

FINISHED SIZE
6.4 x 4.4 x 2.5 cm

➤➤➤ Go

1. Determine the length of the sterling silver wire needed for your desired bracelet size, and then mark and cut the wire. File the ends flat. Anneal the wire if necessary, then pickle and clean.

2. Straighten the wire by gently tapping it with a mallet on a steel block or anvil. Use a permanent marker or scribe to mark the wire into eight even sections.

3. On a steel block with a goldsmithing hammer, flatten the two sections of the wire that are adjacent to the centerline. Watch the wire carefully, counting your hammer blows to keep the wire as even as possible. Use the back of the hammer to add a horizontal texture to the area that was just flattened.

4. Gently hammer the wire ends into a rectangular shape, making sure that both ends are the same thickness.

5. Bend the wire into a figure 8 with one side larger than the other. To accomplish this, place the ends of the wire on opposite sides of the end of the textured area.

6. File the wire ends flush to the center wire, and then solder in place. Pickle and clean.

7. Use a ring mandrel to round out the ends. Use an oval bracelet mandrel to form the cuff.

8. Give the cuff a final finish by brushing it with a brass brush or rubbing it with steel wool.

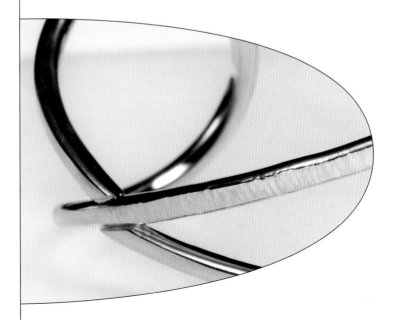

:53

▶ Get Ready

ANNEALING • **SAWING** • **ROLLER PRINTING** • **FILING** • **SOLDERING**
WIREWORK • **FORMING** • **USING LIVER OF SULFUR** • **FINISHING**

▶▶ ▶ Get Set

Copper disk, 14 gauge, 2¾ inches (7 cm)

Sterling silver square wire, 14 gauge, 14 inches (35.6 cm)

Scrap brass round wire, 14 and/or 16 gauge, 2- to 3-inch (5.1 to 7.6 cm) pieces

Bench tool kit, page 9

Soldering kit, page 9

FINISHED SIZE
7.8 x 11.8 x 5.6 cm

▶▶ ▶ Go

1. Anneal the copper disk.

2. Cut various lengths of 14- and/or 16-gauge brass wire for the desired design. Use a rolling mill to print the copper disk with the brass wire design.

3. File the ends of the silver square wire flush, and solder the ends together.

4. Form the wire into a long, skinny oval shape. Use pliers to bend the wire into a funky organic shape, opening the wire in the center to approximately 2½ inches (6.4 cm). Hammer the form around an oval bracelet mandrel.

5. Form the printed copper disk around the same area of the bracelet mandrel to match the curved shape of the wire. Solder the curved wire onto the back of the copper disk.

6. Patina the bracelet using a liver-of-sulfur solution. Sand any excess patina off the bracelet and the silver wire.

7. Tumble the bracelet with steel shot to polish the metal.

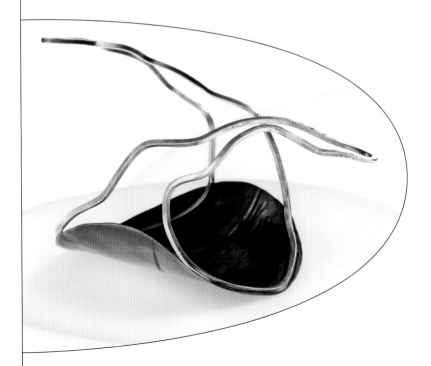

:54

→►▶ **Get Set**

Sterling silver square wire,
2.5 mm, 8¼ inches
(21 cm)

Sterling silver tubing,
6.5 mm ID
(interior diameter),
7.5 mm OD
(outside diameter),
⅝ inch (1.6 cm)

Black acrylic rod, 6.5 mm,
¾ inch (1.9 cm)

Two-part epoxy

Bench tool kit, page 9

Soldering kit, page 9

FINISHED SIZE
6.5 x 5.8 x 1.5 cm

▶▶▶ **Go**

1. Use a saw to cut the 2.5-mm square wire 8¼ inches (21 cm) long.

2. Saw one piece of silver tubing ⁵⁄₁₆ inches (8 mm) long. File the ends flat and smooth.

3. File one edge of the square wire at a 45-degree angle. Using round-nose pliers, make a wire loop that fits around the tubing snugly. Solder the loop closed, pickle, and rinse. File and sand the soldered area. Insert the tubing in the soldered loop, leaving 2 mm extending past one edge.

4. Bend the square wire into an oval by hand first, and then use a wooden mallet and oval bracelet mandrel. Note: At this point, you can change the size of the bracelet by cutting the square wire shorter.

5. File the end of the square wire flat and smooth. Use round-nose pliers to make a curl that perfectly fits around the tubing.

6. Use a square needle file to create a small channel next to the loop soldered in step 3. This channel acts as the clasp catch.

7. Saw a ⅝-inch (1.5 cm) length of acrylic rod. Smooth the cut edges with 1000- or 2000-grit wet sandpaper. Wash and dry the rod. Place a very small amount of epoxy in the tubing, and insert the acrylic piece. Remove any excess epoxy with alcohol, and let dry.

8. Carefully polish the silver to a rouge finish. Note: Too much friction from polishing can melt the acrylic.

:55

▶ Get Ready

SAWING · FILING · SANDING · SOLDERING
FINISHING · SNAP-SETTING LEATHER

▶▶ ▶ Get Set

2 sterling silver disks,
   20 gauge, each
   1⅛ inches (2.86 cm)

2 copper strips, 30 gauge,
   each 1 x ⅛ inch
   (2.5 x 0.3 cm)

Leather, 7½ x ½ inch
   (19 x 1.3 cm)

Hole punch for leather

Snap kit for leather

Bench tool kit, page 9

Soldering kit, page 9

FINISHED SIZE
Metal element,
2.5 x 2.5 x 0.3 cm

▶▶ ▶ Go

1. Draw a line or desired pattern onto one sterling silver disk. Saw along the line to create two pieces for the top of the hollow form. File the cut edges and sand all surfaces.

2. Create a slight curve in the copper pieces using a ring mandrel.

3. Place the copper pieces on the uncut sterling silver disk. Arrange them near the edges of the opposite side of the disk. Make sure there are equal openings on each side that are wide enough for the leather strip. Solder, pickle, and rinse.

4. Place the two pieces created by sawing the first silver disk on the soldering surface. Make sure to separate the pieces enough so there is a ledge for the solder. Place the soldered disk from step 3 on top of the sawed pieces with the copper sandwiched between the silver. Solder, pickle, and rinse.

5. File the metal edges flush. Sand all surfaces to remove burs. Finish the metal with texture wheels on the flexible shaft or with rough sandpaper for a consistent matte finish.

6. Thread the leather strip though the hollow metal form. Punch holes in the leather for the snaps. Follow the directions included with the snap tools to set the snaps on the leather strip.

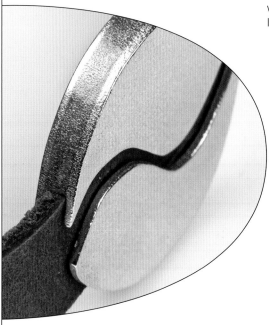

DESIGNER: **ISABELLE LAMONTAGNE**

:56

Get Ready

FILING • FORMING • SAWING • DRILLING • RIVETING
SOLDERING • SANDING • FINISHING

Get Set

Sterling silver square wire,
3.26 x 3.26 mm,
6¾ inches (17.1 cm)

Sterling silver round wire,
13 gauge, 1¼ inches
(3.2 cm)

2 sterling silver strips,
12.5 x 1.63 mm, each
2½ inches (6.4 cm)

Bench tool kit, page 9

Soldering kit, page 9

FINISHED SIZE
2.35 x 6.3 x 3.26 cm

Go

1. File the ends of each sterling silver strip flat. Form the strips around a bracelet mandrel, leaving a flat section on each.

2. Cut the silver square wire into nine pieces: two 1.53-cm lengths, two 1.73-cm lengths, two 1.93-cm lengths, two 2.13-cm lengths, and one 2.33-cm length.

3. Using a 1.83-mm bit, drill a centered hole in the middle of each piece of square wire.

4. Arrange the square wire lengths in the sequence shown in the project photo. Thread the round wire through each square wire. Rivet this arrangement to secure, and then sand the rivet wire ends flush.

5. Solder each end of square-wire component to the flat area of the silver strips. File and sand.

6. Give the bracelet a final finish with a pumice wheel or with steel wool.

APPLYING A HAMMER TEXTURE • FORMING • FILING
WIREWORK • SAWING • GRINDING • SOLDERING • FINISHING
BEZEL SETTING • USING LIVER OF SULFUR

▶ ▶ Get Set

Sterling silver round wire,
   14 gauge, 9 inches
   (22.9 cm)

Sterling silver round bezel
   cup, 6 mm

Flat-back cabochon
   gemstone, 6 mm

4 sterling silver flower
   charms with jump rings,
   each 7 mm

Bench tool kit, page 9

Soldering kit, page 9

FINISHED SIZE
7 x 6.5 cm

▶ ▶ ▶ Go

1. Texture the whole surface of the 9-inch (22.9 cm) length of 14-gauge wire using the small end of a ball-peen hammer.

2. Wrap the textured wire around an oval bracelet mandrel so there is an overlap of approximately 1 inch (2.5 cm). Holding the wire in place on the mandrel, tap all around the wire with a rawhide mallet to shape and strengthen the bracelet.

3. Use pliers to bend one 6-mm segment at one end of the wire into a 90-degree angle. Make sure this small post is protruding vertically. File the end of the post flush.

4. Create a curve in the opposite wire end that will hook around the post made in step 3. Once you have a hook, bend the wire back in the opposite direction, creating a second curve. (The end of the wire should now re-semble an S. The lower curve in the S is the hook-closure for the bangle, while the upper curve acts as a seat for soldering on the flower.) Trim any excess wire at the top of the S, and file flush.

5. Cut the jump ring off the back of one flower charm. Using a heatless grinding wheel on a flexible shaft, grind down the back of the flower, creating a level surface. Use a center punch to make a small divot on the back of the bezel cup.

6. Secure the bangle in a third hand with the S hook facing up. Solder the flower in place. Pickle, rinse, and brass brush the bangle. Slide the remaining three flower charms onto the bangle.

7. Place the bezel cup face down on the soldering surface. Secure the bangle, post down, in a third hand. Solder the post to the back of the bezel cup. Pickle, rinse, and brass brush the bangle.

8. Set the stone in the bezel. Patina the bangle using liver of sulfur, and then polish.

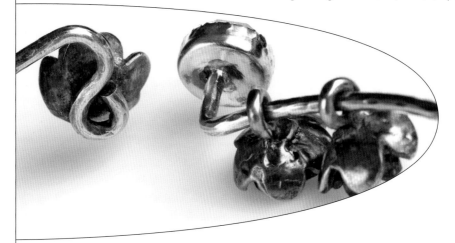

:58

Get Ready

SAWING · FILING · FORMING · APPLYING A HAMMER TEXTURE
SOLDERING · DRILLING · POLISHING · BALLING WIRE

▸▸ ▸ **Get Set**

Sterling silver round wire,
8 gauge, 4½ inches
(11.4 cm)

Sterling silver round wire,
18 gauge, 4 inches
(10.2 cm)

Sterling silver flat wire,
2 x 3 mm, 2 inches
(5.1 cm)

Sterling silver tubing,
1.6 mm OD (outside
diameter)

2 faceted garnet beads,
each 10 to 12 mm

Bench tool kit, page 9

Soldering kit, page 9

Diamond drill bit, 1.7 mm

FINISHED SIZE
6.4 x 5.7 cm

▸▸ ▸ **Go**

1. Measure and cut a 4¾-inch (12 cm) length of 8-gauge sterling silver wire. File the wire ends flat.

2. Measure and cut two pieces of the sterling silver flat wire, each 2 inches (5.1 cm) long. Mark the center of each piece with a scribe.

3. Using a mallet and a dapping punch that is about the same diameter as the beads, form the flat wire into a U shape at the center line, creating even lengths on both sides. Texture the sides of the wire with a chasing tool or hammer.

4. Solder the center of each U-shape wire to one end of the 8-gauge silver wire.

5. Round the tips of the ends of the U arms with a file or a cup burr. Measure and mark 3 mm down from each end of each U arm. Drill a centered hole at each marked point using a 1-mm bit.

6. Form the cuff around an oval bracelet mandrel. Polish the cuff to the desired finish.

7. Measure and cut two lengths of the sterling silver tubing. Each tube should fit snugly between the two arms of the U-shaped wires.

8. Enlarge the holes in the garnet beads with a 1.7-mm diamond bit. Feed a piece of tubing through the hole in each bead, and insert the bead between its silver U arms.

9. Cut two 1-inch (2.5 cm) lengths of 18-gauge sterling silver wire. Ball one end of each wire with a torch. Pickle and polish each ball.

10. Insert one balled wire through one U arm, tubing, and bead, and snip off the wire, leaving a 3- to 4-mm tail. Ball this wire tail with a torch, making sure not to heat the bead. Repeat this step for the second U arm.

:59

▶▶ **Get Set**

Sterling silver round wire,
18 gauge, 5½ feet
(1.67 m)

Brass round wire,
18 gauge, 13 inches
(33 cm)

Bench tool kit, page 9

FINISHED SIZE
22 x 9 x 0.25 cm

DESIGNER'S NOTE
These instructions make a
five-bracelet set.

▶▶▶ **Go**

1. Adjust the width between the rollers of the rolling mill to slightly flatten the round silver wire. (You may want to flatten a small test piece of wire first to get the width just right.) Run the entire length of silver wire through the rolling mill. Without changing the width between the rollers, roll the entire length of brass wire through the mill.

2. Measure and cut 25 lengths of silver wire, each approximately 2½ inches (6.4 cm) long. (These lengths can be varied slightly.) Measure and cut five lengths of brass wire, each approximately 2½ inches (6.4 cm) long. These lengths can also be varied slightly.

3. File each wire end flush, and remove any burrs.

4. Using round-nose pliers, bend a closed loop on both ends of each wire. Important: Bend one wire end in one direction and the other end in the opposite direction.

5. Connect the looped ends of four silver links to form a chain. Repeat to make five separate chains.

6. Make a hot liver-of-sulfur bath, and patina all five chains. Brush the chains with a brass brush to clean.

7. Use one brass link to connect one oxidized silver chain from end to end, forming a bracelet. Repeat this step to create a set of five bracelets.

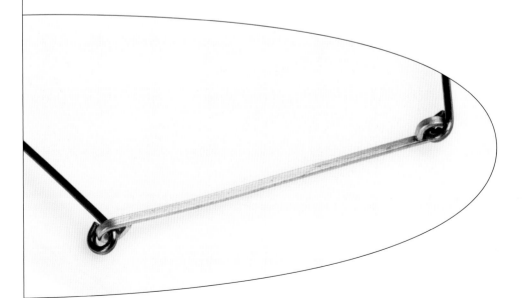

:60

▶▶ ▶ Get Set

Sterling silver square wire,
3 mm, 5 inches
(12.7 cm)

Sterling silver tubing,
5 mm OD (outside
diameter)

Sterling silver round wire,
18 gauge, 1¼ inches
(3.2 cm)

6 14-karat gold balls with
one hole, each 3 mm

Bench tool kit, page 9

Soldering kit, page 9

FINISHED SIZE
8 x 4.5 x 1.9 cm

▶▶ ▶ Go

1. Determine the length of sterling silver square wire needed for your desired bracelet size. For an average-size bracelet, mark and cut the metal 5 inches (12.5 cm) long. File the ends of the wire flat. Using a wooden mallet and an oval bracelet mandrel, bend the wire into a half-oval.

2. Mark and saw two pieces of silver tubing, each 3¼ inches (8.3 cm) long. File the cut ends flat and smooth.

3. Saw a piece of silver square wire 5 mm long. Sand each end of the wire flat and even. Measure and mark a centerline on each piece of silver tubing. Solder the 5-mm piece of square wire between the two lengths of tubing in the center. Pickle, rinse, and dry.

4. Insert the square wire bent in step 1 into the soldered pieces of tubing. Mark the tubing in the center, where each edge of the square wire rests. Dimple and drill a 1-mm hole straight through each piece.

5. Hinge one end of the bracelet by inserting the 18-gauge round wire into the holes of the tubing, the square wire, and the tubing on the opposite side. Use snips to cut off the excess silver wire, leaving about 1 mm poking out. Place a gold ball on the end of each wire, and solder in place. Pickle and rinse.

6. On the opposite end, insert the 18-gauge silver wire through the holes drilled in each length of tubing. Snip off any extra wire, leaving about 1 mm on each side. Solder a gold ball on each wire. Pickle and rinse.

7. Use a 1-mm cylindrical burr to cut a notch in the square wire to use as a catch.

8. Solder the last two gold balls in place on the outside of the tubing in the middle of the bracelet. Pickle, rinse, and dry.

9. Sand the bracelet, and then polish it to a rouge finish.

CONTRIBUTING DESIGNERS

Elena Bonanomi lives in Milan, Italy, and works as a jewelry designer and goldsmith. Her works, characterized by simple and linear shapes, use traditional jewelry materials, like silver, gems, pearls, and colored thread. She also explores the possibilities of moving elements and mutation of forms in space. Visit her website at www.elenabonanomi.blogspot.com.

Based in Sydney, Australia, **Fairina Cheng** recently received her diploma in jewelry and object design. This was an unexpected career path, inspired by an offhand decision to take a nighttime jewelry class. She is loving every bit of the journey and learning more and more that sometimes the best decisions are those made by chance.

Sunyoung Cheong is a metalsmith and jewelry designer living in Topeka, Kansas. His work is focused on body adornment, primarily using techniques such as fabrication, casting, enameling, and CAD. He often incorporates textiles and fiber techniques into his jewelry designs.

Natsumi Comstock is a jewelry designer working and living in San Francisco, California, where she studied at the Revere Academy of Jewelry Arts. She enjoys working with Argentium silver and recycled materials. You can view more of her work at www.tsunagujewelry.com.

Aimee Domash is a St. Louis, Missouri-based art jeweler who works mostly with silver: sterling, Argentium, and fine. She adds color to her designs with gold, enamel, gemstones, resin, plastic, and sometimes even handmade paper. She enjoys making elegant and clean-lined jewelry as well as more traditional pieces. Visit her websites at www.aimeedomash.com and www.salmonrockstudio.com.

Rachel M. Dow is a studio artist who has always been drawn to nature and found objects. Her art is focused on metal fabrication and hand-dyed and handspun fiber yarn. Her work is shown in selected galleries and online at www.rmddesigns.com.

Aja Engel attended the University of Nebraska-Lincoln, where she studied printmaking and painting. She currently works in the metalsmithing studio at Lill Street Art Center in Chicago, Illionois, where she continues exploring etching on metal, textures, and color. You can find her work at www.ajaengel.com.

Deborah Fehrenbach teaches locally in Michigan and is a working jewelry designer and goldsmith. She can be contacted at deborahmarie@mutualdata.com.

Beatriz Fortez has had a life-long love affair with jewelry and its mixture of simple beauty and symbolic meaning. From concept and design to fabrication, she says the process of creating a piece combines creativity, aesthetic, and skill.

Michele Grady has been working with metals for more than 22 years. She teaches classes and workshops in art centers and galleries, as well as in her own studio. Her work is sold at craft shows and in many galleries throughout the United States.

Denise Harrison was born and raised in Honolulu, Hawaii, where her grandmother was always pointing out the patterns made by nature in the sand, the tree roots, the leaves—everywhere. In fall 2007 she stumbled upon a metals program in Oregon and was immediately hooked. You can see more of her work, which combines photography and silversmithing, at www.sterlingechoes.com or in Lark Jewelry & Beading's *30-Minute Rings* and *Chains Chains Chains*.

Susan Holmes was born in Leeds, Yorkshire, in northern England, and now lives in the Morvan regional park in Burgundy, France. She has always enjoyed craftwork, notably sewing and knitting, and is mastering the techniques of beading and stringing.

Kelly Jones of Wraptillion started an industrial jewelry design business from unusual hardware. She transforms American-manufactured hardware components and titanium waste from the aerospace industry into sculptural pieces with strong, delicate lines and intricate movement. Her jewelry can be found in boutiques, galleries, and museum shops. Visit her website at www.wraptillion.com.

Isabelle LaMontagne graduated in 2008 from CEGEP's jewelry program in Quebec City, Canada. Her goal is to create jewels that can be modified and worn in more than one way. Visit her website at www.isabellelamontagne.com.

Karen J. Lauseng is an internationally recognized New Mexico artist whose work has been published by Lark Jewelry & Beading, *Art Jewelry Magazine*, *Lapidary Journal Jewelry Artist*, and Creative Home Arts Club. She has displayed her pieces in more than 100 venues, including solo exhibitions, juried shows, and galleries. See her work at www.kjartworks.com.

Nancy Lee makes contemporary art jewelry and sculpture from metal. She exhibits and sells work from her gallery, Nancy Lee Designs, and at local and national galleries and teaches jewelry making for the metalsmith. See more at www.ndesignsmetal.com.

A goldsmith and designer for the past 20 years, Ottawa, Canada, native **Ann L. Lumsden** has striven to create both contemporary and classic pieces. Through exploration of traditional and avant-garde materials and techniques, her work keeps evolving. She is a member of the Metal Arts Guild of Canada, and her work has won Best in Show twice in the guild's annual juried exhibition.

Amy Proff Lyons is an artist, a wife to one incredibly patient man, and a mother to three whiz-bang kids. She never met an art medium she didn't like. Don't ask her to choose a favorite— seriously, it would be like asking her to choose a favorite child.

Susan Machamer is a professional metalsmith, designer, and gemologist living in upstate New York. She enjoys designing one-of-a-kind jewelry pieces using fine metals and unusual gemstones. Susan's work has a strong connection to natural forms and textures.

Joseph Naskar is an interior designer, photographer, jewelry designer, and beader. He is a strong advocate for developing new techniques that are challenging and ideas that are innovative. "Let's tear down walls daily, so that all the usual rules won't be our prisons," he says. See more and interact at www.3stolenbeads.com.

Lia Paletta graduated in 2009 in product design from the University of the State of Minas Gerais in Brazil and studied goldsmithing in Brazil and Mexico. Today, she is an associate of the design firm Gabbo Design, which offers integrated graphic and product design and works particularly with jewelry and fashion accessories.

Elizabeth Payne is a designer and metalsmith whose path to the craft of jewelry making has included formal illustration training, direct learning from many gifted and generous instructors, and lots of practice. She lives with her husband and two boys in sunny Southern California. To learn more about Elizabeth, visit www.jewelryartsstudio.com.

Erin Prais-Hintz designs one-of-a-kind jewelry in Stevens Point, Wisconsin, where she lives with her husband and children. Collaboration is key to Erin's creativity, and she enjoys nothing more than connecting with other artists and telling stories through her wearable art. Read about Erin's creative adventures at www.treasures-found.blogspot.com.

Kat Roberts lives in Brooklyn, New York, where she works as an artist, designer, and footwear instructor. She regularly contributes to BurdaStyle, and she chronicles her obsession with creative recycling in her blog www.wecanredoit.blogspot.com.

John Sartin is an award-winning metalsmith and jewelry artist who has been crafting exquisite wearable sculpture since 2002. His work has been featured in and graced the covers of leading trade magazines and publications. He currently resides in Albuquerque, New Mexico.

Brenda Schweder is the author of *Steel Wire Jewelry* (Lark Beading & Jewelry) *Vintage Redux* and, *Junk to Jewelry*. Between her jewelry designs and Fashion Forecasts, Schweder has been published more than 100 times. Visit her at www.facebook.com/brenda.schweder or www.brendaschweder.com.

Rachel Sims is a world-travelling, book-devouring, street-treasure-finding, Rhode Island School of Design-educated glass artist and silversmith with a penchant for quirky design. She left designing luxury watches in Switzerland to move back to Iowa to create jewelry and teach workshops. Her work can be seen at http://fuzzi-shu.etsy.com, and a full list of classes can be found at www.fuzzishu.com

Theresa St. Romain is a metalsmith and jewelry artist living in Atlanta, Georgia. She teaches at the Spruill Center for the Arts in Atlanta and Pratt Fine Arts Center in Seattle, Washington. Her work can be seen at Topaz Gallery in Atlanta and at www.saintromain.com.

Victoria L. Takahashi says, "I love to create—it is my only true passion. I am forever grateful to have my life filled with supportive people and unlimited inspiration. I hope that following my dreams will help others have the courage to do so."

Amy Tavern is a studio jeweler and educator who lives and works in Penland, North Carolina. Her work is sold around the United States and is featured in several Lark Jewelry & Beading books, including *30-Minute Necklaces* and *500 Silver Jewelry Designs*. For more information please visit www.amytavern.com and www.amytavern.blogspot.com.

Victoria Tillotson is a jewelry designer and professor of jewelry making at the School of Visual Arts in New York City. She authored *Chic Metal* and contributed to *30-Minute Necklaces* and *30-Minute Rings*. Her jewelry has been in *Allure*, *Lucky*, *Essence*, and *Complex*, as well as on MTV, Oxygen, and HSN. See more of Victoria's work at www.victoriatillotson.com.

Joanne Tinley began her professional life as a secondary school teacher but always made jewelry, partly to relax after work. She began to sell her jewelry regularly, and people asked her to teach them jewelry making, so she became a jewelry designer and tutor. A regular contributor to British craft magazines and a City & Guilds jewelry design teacher at a local college, Joanne lives with her family in Southampton, England.

John Tzelepis received his undergraduate degree from Skidmore College and his MFA in Metals from Arizona State University. He has made jewelry and sculpture for more than a decade, exhibited work nationally, and been featured in several publications. You can see his work at www.johntzelepis.com.

Ingeborg Vandamme is a jewelry designer from the Netherlands. She works and lives in Amsterdam, where she studied jewelry at Gerrit Rietveld Academy. Ingeborg experiments with a combination of materials, like paper, textiles, and metal. Her work is in magazines and books, including many by Lark Jewelry & Beading. Visit her website at www.ingeborgvandamme.nl.

Federico Vianello started making jewelry in the 1980s in Florence, Italy, where he opened his first workshop (see www.microfficina.com). He teaches the theory, practice, and technology of jewelry making and design. He writes, "Thesis and antithesis: everything is by chance/nothing is by chance; the space between things is what really intrigues me."

Vanessa Walilko is a jewelry designer and wearable art maker. Her beadwork and chain-mail designs have taken top honors in the Bead Dreams competition, the Jewelry Arts Awards, and the British Bead Awards and have been in national exhibitions at the Museum of Fine Arts, Houston, and the Indianapolis Museum of Art. Visit her website at www.kalibutterfly.com.

Nancy Wickman started designing wire jewelry in 2006. She lives in Flushing, Michigan, with her four Boston Terriers. Nancy teaches classes and sells her work at shows and at www.wickwirejewelry.artfire.com.

Kimberley Williamson-Fistler is owner of Twisted Sisters Crafting in downtown Cedar Falls, Iowa. She says she loves teaching her customers that "creating art feeds the soul. Everybody has art within them. It just takes some coaxing out with the right tools and instructions and a little inspiration." Kimberley's favorite crafts are lampworking and jewelry making.

Jaesun Won earned his MFA in Metal and Jewelry Design from the School for American Crafts at Rochester Institute of Technology in 2007. He was a NICHE Awards winner in Professional Fine Jewelry in 2010. He also contributed work to Lark Jewelry & Beading's *500 Silver Jewelry Designs*.

Carole Zakkour grew up in Beirut, Lebanon, moved to the United States to pursue her studies, and then decided to become a self-taught jeweler. She loves to travel, and she is inspired by science, nature, and various cultures. She lives in Venice, California, and can be reached at www.carolezakkour.com

ABOUT THE AUTHOR

Marthe Le Van is a jewelry, metals, and beading editor for Lark Jewelry & Beading. Since 2000, she has written, edited, juried, or curated more than 60 books. Recent publications include the first three titles in this series, *30-Minute Earrings*, *30-Minute Necklaces*, and *30-Minute Rings*. Marthe has edited all the jewelry books in Lark's popular "500" series and curated *Ring a Day*, *21st Century Jewelry*, *500 Wedding Rings*, and *Masters: Gold*. She is a member of the Art Jewelry Forum and the Society of North American Goldsmiths.

ACKNOWLEDGMENTS

Lark Jewelry & Beading has received a wonderful outpouring of support for the 30-Minute series of books, and we are grateful for the enthusiasm of the jewelry and craft community! We feel so fortunate to collaborate with incredible jewelry designers from all around the world. *30-Minute Bracelets* features original projects created in Australia, Brazil, Canada, France, Italy, the Netherlands, Scotland, South Korea, United Kingdom, and the United States. In case you're not counting, that's 10 countries on five continents. On behalf of the entire jewelry team, I thank all the designers for contributing their ideas, expertise, and precious time. Your dedication never wavers, and your extraordinary effort does not go unnoticed.

I can't say enough about the unbelievably dedicated team that worked on *30-Minute Bracelets*. Many thanks to designer Kay Stafford, who did a stellar job with the layout and cover design, and to Kristi Pfeffer, whose artistic vision for this series has led us to great success. Thanks to Stewart O'Shields for his sparkling and clear photography, and to art director Kathy Holmes for her expert eye and styling. Joanna Gollberg excelled as the technical editor for this book. Thank you for your outstanding skill and dedication. With enviable efficiency and grace, Abby Haffelt, Hannah Doyle, and Carol Barnao provided much-appreciated editorial and art support. I'm grateful for their help.

Finally, I'd like to thank our readers for the passion they have for our books. I hope these designs, once again, bring you hours of joy (but only in 30-minute increments). We do it for you!

DESIGNER INDEX

240 INVENTIVE AND FUN PROJECTS FOR JEWELERS!

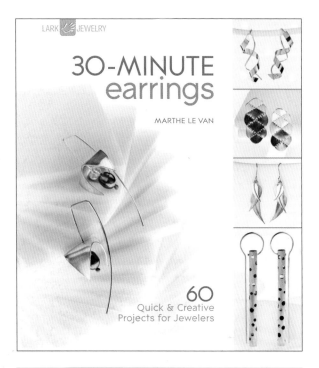

LARK JEWELRY

30-MINUTE
earrings

MARTHE LE VAN

60
Quick & Creative
Projects for Jewelers

LARK JEWELRY

30-MINUTE
necklaces

MARTHE LE VAN

60
Quick & Creative
Projects for Jewelers

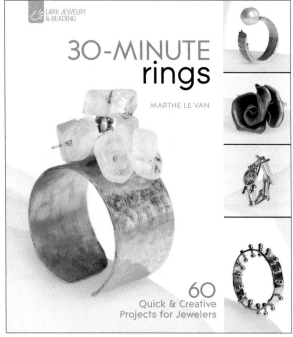

LARK JEWELRY & BEADING

30-MINUTE
rings

MARTHE LE VAN

60
Quick & Creative
Projects for Jewelers

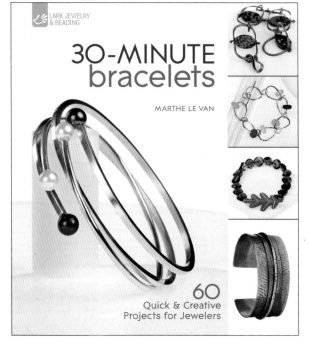

LARK JEWELRY & BEADING

30-MINUTE
bracelets

MARTHE LE VAN

60
Quick & Creative
Projects for Jewelers